UNWRITTEN

Bat Flips, the Fun Police, and Baseball's New Future

Danny Knobler

Library of Congress Catalog-in-Publication Data available upon request.

This book is available in quantity at special discounts for your group or organization. For further information, contact:

Triumph Books LLC
814 North Franklin Street
Chicago, Illinois 60610
(312) 337–0747
www.triumphbooks.com

Printed in U.S.A.
ISBN: 978-1-62937-648-6
Design by Meghan Grammer
Page production by Nord Compo

CONTENTS

INTRODUCTION

What Are the Unwritten Rules...
and What Happened to Them?

YASIEL PUIG LEARNED HIS BASEBALL IN CUBA. KENTA MAEDA grew up in Japan. Kenley Jansen comes from Curacao.

In every one of those countries, the rules of baseball are the same. Three strikes, you're out. Circle the bases, you score a run. Nine batters in the lineup, nine innings in a regulation game.

It's all in the rulebook, everything from 1.00, Objectives of the Game (win by scoring more runs than the opponent), to 9.23 (d), Suspended Games (all performances shall be considered as occurring on the original date of the game).

It's all in there... except the part that tells you when it's alright to flip your bat... and the part about when it's acceptable to retaliate when your teammate(s) get hit by a pitch... and when no one will have a problem with you bunting for a hit... or speaking to a pitcher who hasn't yet allowed a hit.

There's more, because the unwritten rules of the game are nearly as extensive as the written ones.

This isn't the NFL, where the rulebook determines how and where you can celebrate, and what you can use as a prop. In baseball, the players decide that. Cross the line, and your teammates will let you know. Cross the line by too much and the opponent will let you know, with a 99 mph fastball to the ribs.

The unwritten rules tell you how the game really should be played, both at the major-league level and while you're coming up through the minor leagues. Everyone who wants to play the game right has to learn them. Every fan who wants to watch the game and fully understand it should know them.

The only problem is the unwritten rules change over time. The written rules change, too, but Major League Baseball publishes a new version of the rulebook every year with changes noted.

The unwritten rules change more gradually. They change as society changes. They change as the players change. They become the reason some guys get called "old school" and some don't.

There was a time when rookies were expected to shut up and "know their place." Not true anymore.

There was a time when playing for one run made perfect sense, so teams used the sacrifice bunt with regularity. Definitely not true anymore.

There was a time when as soon as the leadoff man in an inning reached first base, you'd wonder if the manager would put on a hit-and-run play. Now, the hit-and-run is so rare that when I asked major-league scouts how often they'd seen it done in a full season, most said they could count the number on one hand.

There was also a time when a pitcher might throw at a hitter simply for taking a big swing, and certainly for taking a little extra time getting around the bases on a home run. It was expected, and perhaps even accepted, that a hitter who had great success against a certain pitcher could expect a brushback pitch to come his way soon.

The few times that happens now, it becomes a major controversy and the pitcher who does it gets criticized and suspended.

"In today's game, I think there's a mutual respect," said Chili Davis, who debuted as a major-league player in 1981 and has been around the game as a player or coach ever since. "Guys don't throw at guys because they beat them."

Pitchers throw harder than ever now, but when you ask scouts and coaches how often they've seen one of today's pitchers use intimidation as a weapon, many of them say, "Never, at least not intentionally." If a pitcher comes far inside, it's often because his command just isn't very good and he missed his spot.

Oh, and that starting pitcher? There's a good chance he won't make it three times through the opposing batting order. That's a big change, because in the game as it was played 20 and especially 30 years ago, a manager wouldn't go to the bullpen if he had a lead and his starter was still throwing the ball well and getting hitters out.

In 2018, several teams regularly began games with an "opener," a pitcher who was designated to throw the first inning or perhaps the first and second innings. The Tampa Bay Rays didn't have a traditional five-man rotation at any point during the season.

It wasn't a rules change that brought that about. It was more of a culture change, a change to what smart baseball people thought.

The embrace of analytics and all forms of big data has changed the game and changed the definition of playing the game right. Many analytics-inclined fans and even executives wish and hope that it will change more, especially in areas like bullpen usage.

Today's general managers are more open to change than ever. Today's managers are, too, even some you might think of as decidedly "old school." Bob Melvin admits now that he was resistant to analytics when the Diamondbacks new front office turned to them heavily in 2006. He became so comfortable with the new methods that in 2018 he was in his eighth year with the Oakland Athletics, working for Billy Beane of *Moneyball* fame and using an opener rather than a traditional starting pitcher regularly in a pennant race.

Don Mattingly never seemed completely comfortable with the Dodgers after Andrew Friedman took over baseball operations and big data dictated decisions beginning in 2015. But in 2018, when Mattingly was managing the Miami Marlins, he didn't brush away a question about whether he would consider using an opener.

"I don't think you'll see us doing that," Mattingly said. "But I think you have to be open-minded to anything. Analytics, shifting... you have to evolve with the game. You should never close your mind to anything. I've always heard that you're looking for the best way, not looking for your way."

That's a long way from, "It's either my way or the highway and we're going to weed out the rats," as Hall of Fame manager Sparky Anderson told his team when he took over the Tigers in 1979.

Anderson was a brilliant manager, several steps and several innings ahead of most of those he managed against. But he was also the guy who once said, "If I need a computer, it means I don't have a brain."

Computers are standard for just about all of us now, and laptops, smartphones, tablets, and even smart watches are a common sight in any manager's office. The information generated by computers shows up every night in every major-league dugout and influences nearly every decision made in every game.

So of course the unwritten rules have had to change. But they didn't disappear.

Baseball commissioner Rob Manfred acknowledged as much at a press conference in 2016. Asked how he felt about celebrations, bat flips, and the like, Manfred said the players determine how the game should be played.

"Overall, baseball has always had unwritten rules that kind of govern what's appropriate and what's not appropriate," Manfred said. "The way I think about the changes we've seen in the last couple of years, is that we have a really exciting, new, young generation in the game. And just like the players 20 years ago, they are going to develop a set of unwritten rules as to what's acceptable and what's not."

Plenty of players and more than a few managers wish Manfred and other executives would stick to the idea that players can govern the game themselves. Many of them believe baseball has gone too far with changes in the official rules and with heavier suspensions for what they see as simply "policing the game."

Changes in the official rules have affected the unwritten rules. Baseball has basically outlawed collisions at home plate and hard slides to break up a double play, taking away what once would have been considered essentials for "playing the game the right way."

The use of instant replay to uphold or overturn umpire calls has changed the interaction between players, managers, and umps. Disputes remain, especially over balls and strikes, and even that could change if baseball ever goes to robot umps or some other form of strike-zone technology to make those decisions. But arguments, ejections, and working the umpires aren't nearly as big a part of the game as they were before.

In a July 2018 segment on FanCred, former major-league player and manager Bobby Valentine was asked what he would do if he were made commissioner.

"The first thing I'd do is take away that rule at second base [on potential double plays]," said Valentine, who played both shortstop and second base during his career. "The most athletic play you ever saw on a baseball diamond was a double play. The second baseman, the shortstop, the shortstop coming across, doing a ballet step as he dodges the runner in midair, throws a strike to first base and then might roll on the ground as he's doing it. That's the true athletic play of baseball, and that was taken away from the game.... I think that that was the biggest mistake baseball has ever made."

Valentine also bemoaned the way instant replay has cut down on ejections and arguments. The fans loved those, he said.

So did he. Valentine, remember, was the New York Mets manager who was ejected from a 1999 game, then came back to the dugout wearing a fake mustache and dark glasses.

The prevalence of social media has changed the game in other ways. Players are more accessible to fans than ever, except that accessibility over the Internet has led many of them to guard their actual private time and lives even more closely.

Puig and Maeda and Jansen and every other player who comes to the big leagues quickly learn that the unwritten rules matter. Follow them and you win acceptance from players, officials, and fans. Fail to learn them or decide to ignore them and people will be talking about you, and not in a nice way.

Just because you can play the game one way in Havana, Tokyo, or Willemstad, that doesn't mean the same will be celebrated in New York, Boston, or Chicago. Or in Los Angeles, where Puig, Maeda, and Jansen helped take the Dodgers to the 2017 and '18 World Series.

As Martin Prado put it, "Just because you walk around your own house in your underwear, that doesn't mean you can walk into your neighbor's house and do the same thing."

Prado, who grew up in Venezuela and signed with the Atlanta Braves when he was 17 years old, learned the unwritten rules so well that he became one of the game's most respected veterans. He learned from his teammates and he tries to pass on what he knows to the young players he comes in contact with.

Those players learn the unwritten rules over time. Some are lucky enough that they had fathers or other relatives who played the game at a high level. Others had influential coaches in high school, in college, in the minor leagues, or in their early years in the majors. Even more of them relied on teammates. Those players learn the rules, and then as a group they adapt them to their time and their cultural norms. Since it's the players who police the unwritten rules, it's also the players who tend to adjust them. It's not all in their hands, because managers make decisions and more often than ever front-office people do, too.

They will all pass the rules on to the next generation. And then some of those rules will change again.

1

Respect the Game,
and Play to Win

IT DIDN'T TAKE LONG FOR JUSTIN VERLANDER TO REALIZE
how fortunate he was.

Fortunate that the fading Detroit Tigers decided to trade him
in August of 2017. Fortunate that the Houston Astros, after not
showing much interest either at the July 31 non-waiver trade
deadline or through almost all of August, decided on the final
day of the month that Verlander was the missing piece in their
carefully built puzzle.

Verlander was fortunate no team had put in a waiver claim,
which would, in effect, have kept the Tigers from trading him
that month. And also that when the Tigers came to him to seek
his approval—he had full no-trade protection—he agreed to the
deal. It went right down to the last minute—even the last seconds,
Verlander would say later—but he said yes.

It was a fortunate decision, and not just because two months
later Verlander would be celebrating the first World Series
championship of his 13-year major-league career.

It was more than that. It was that Verlander had stumbled onto a team that played the game of baseball the way he played it, that followed the game's unwritten rules as he had learned them. "This team does," Verlander said, after he had been with the Astros for nearly a full year. "Everybody [with the Astros] does."

The Astros, for all their young talent and new-school embrace of analytics, were still old school when it came to the things that mattered most. They still believed in playing the game hard and playing it right, in respecting the game and respecting their opponents.

And most of all, they believed in playing to win.

The best teams still do, even if many of the details of how they do it have changed. Baseball has legislated against hard takeouts at second base and bowling over the catcher to try to score a run. The high-and-tight fastball as an attempt to intimidate has more or less left the game. Beanball wars are much less common, with at least one major-league manager telling his pitchers he doesn't believe in intentionally throwing at batters. What once would have been seen as over-the-top celebrations are accepted without a second thought, and rookies come to the big leagues without even once being told to sit down, shut up, and know your place.

The details have changed. The bigger picture hasn't.

Talk to prominent major leaguers, from veterans like Verlander to kids like Aaron Judge and Juan Soto, and one of the words you hear most often is "respect."

"You always ask yourself, 'Is it disrespectful to my teammates? Is it disrespectful to the game?'" said Walt Weiss, who played 14 seasons in the major leagues and later coached and managed.

Respect the game. Respect the uniform and the organization it represents. Respect your teammates, but also your opponents.

"I respect people who respect me," said Javier Baez, an emerging star with the Chicago Cubs.

Winning teams and winning players do all of that. Verlander found all of that when he came to the Astros, who were 80–53 the day he arrived.

And rather than the culture being the result of the winning, Verlander came to believe it was the other way around.

"I think it's the cause of winning," he said. "When everybody comes in, no matter whether you've got one day [of service time in the big leagues] or 15 years, you know everybody is there to kick the other team's ass every day. That's the only reason you're here. It's a different feeling. The best teams do [have that]."

The team Verlander left in Detroit was no longer one of the best. The Tigers had gone to the World Series twice and the postseason two other times in Verlander's first nine seasons. but the team he left had a 58–74 record, on the way to 98 losses.

The Tigers under Jim Leyland had been one of the teams that did things the right way. Leyland demanded it, and he was able to get his players to buy into it.

Verlander found that the Astros under A.J. Hinch were the same way. So did Gerrit Cole, when he arrived from the Pittsburgh Pirates after a January 2018 trade.

"It's 25 guys playing extremely hard every day," Cole said. "That's kind of an understatement. It boils down to having players with talent, but there's a focus, a preparation that goes into the mindset to be able to go all out."

Cole pointed to Astros right fielder Josh Reddick.

"That guy drills the cutoff man right in the chest, even if it's the third double in a row you've given up down the line," he said. "He gives that same effort as he gave the first one. You throw someone out, or you hold them from taking the extra 90 feet, and it can change the whole course of a game."

The team Verlander and Cole described was the one that won the 2017 World Series, but they just as easily could have been describing a championship team from the 1950s, '80s, or early 2000s. The game has changed, in many ways, but just because the Astros shift a lot on defense and rarely use the bunt doesn't mean they reinvented the most important things about how the game is played.

Neither did the Cubs, the team that won its first World Series in 108 years in 2016.

"I feel like you have 25 guys just going in the same direction," said Jason Heyward, who signed with the Cubs as a free agent in December 2015. "Regardless of why they want to win, they're just trying to win. This team, right away it was easy to see that guys just wanted to be a part of helping, do whatever they can on a given night to help. Whatever it was, they were just trying to find a way to help. If you didn't get your chance, you were itching for the next chance.

"At the end of the day, once you become a winning team and are expected to win, guys are going to bring it even more."

Heyward learned early what it meant to play the right way. He grew up in Georgia in the middle of the Braves' 14-year run as division champions. His mother is from New York, and Heyward came of age during the Yankees' championship run of the late 1990s.

Derek Jeter was his favorite player. He watched Chipper Jones all the time and eventually shared a clubhouse with him after being drafted and signed by the Braves.

"When you have Chipper Jones take you off to the side and tell you, 'We go about things this way or that way,' you learn," Heyward said. "I always try to hustle. I don't show people up. That's just me. That's how I am."

Heyward worries that etiquette isn't as common in baseball as it was when he watched as a kid or when he debuted in 2010.

"But I think people in the game still do appreciate the old-school way or the old-fashioned way," he said.

It's not just old managers and older fans, either. It's not just former players sitting in the broadcast booth and celebrating when they see a pitcher work inside or a batter calmly put his bat down and run the bases after hitting a home run.

It's guys like Heyward, and also his Cubs teammate Kris Bryant, who makes a point of never flipping his bat.

"That dude's an MVP all the way around," Heyward said. "The way he does it. Hustles, everything."

The best players and the best teams still do.

2

When Numbers Change the Game

I DIDN'T WANT THIS BOOK TO BE ENTIRELY ABOUT NUMBERS, but it's impossible to write about the way baseball has changed without acknowledging the effect of analytics. More numbers than ever are available, and more smart people than ever are joining baseball front offices and figuring out ways to turn those numbers into wins.

There's more willingness than ever to challenge traditional norms, to avoid doing something simply because it's the way we've always done it.

"We should always be open to changing our minds," said Philadelphia Phillies manager Gabe Kapler, who is as new school as they come but is perfectly willing to listen if you want to make the argument his methods won't work.

Baseball has always been something of copycat game, and anytime one team succeeds doing something different, there's a rush of other teams trying to do the same thing. But there's also room for a smart guy trying to buck the trend, whether it's Earl

Weaver preferring three-run home runs to playing for one run in the 1970s or Billy Beane seeking out players with high on-base percentages in the early 2000s.

The copycat crowd now is all-in with analytics, preferably with an Ivy League general manager in place, a heavy reliance on defensive shifts, and a roster chosen based more on what the numbers and algorithms say than on what the general manager hears from scouts in the field. The numbers dictate matchups and often the daily lineups, and the numbers influence pitch selection.

The Moneyball trends that began with Beane and the Oakland A's aren't outliers, but Beane found other ways to go against the norm and get his low-budget team to the 2018 playoffs. The defensive trends that began with Joe Maddon, when his 2010 Tampa Bay Rays used defensive shifts 221 times—88 more than anyone else in the majors that season—have now gone far beyond anything Maddon imagined. Maddon's Chicago Cubs shifted about 40 percent more times than his 2010 Rays (315 times, according to Statcast), but instead of ranking a distant first, they ranked 28th among the 30 teams. The Houston Astros had shifted 2,196 times, seven times as often as the Cubs.

The increased use of shifts and overall better defensive positioning has made it harder for hitters to get ground balls through the infield, helping to convince more and more hitters that their best route to success is to increase their launch angle and hit more balls in the air. Perhaps someday it will lead to more emphasis on hitters using all fields, making them harder to shift against, but so far more seem intent on hitting the ball over the fence, figuring no shift can stop a home run.

Analytics aren't going away, nor should they. Any team should want to make use of as much information as is available, and modern teams have access to far more than their predecessors did. Shifts are far easier to design, for example, because instead of relying on spray charts compiled by hand, teams can now look at every ball a player has ever hit and where it went, and break it down by the count and type of pitch.

Statcast, which uses high-resolution optical cameras and radar equipment, tracks the location of the ball and of every player through each and every major-league game. Teams (and fans) have more accurate measures of a player's speed than was ever available before, along with spin rates for every pitch, how direct a route an outfielder takes to a fly ball, and tons of other data.

Teams develop proprietary software that attempts to project how players will perform. Some teams have become so dependent on those projections that they have few if any scouts watching professional games in person to evaluate players for free agency or trades.

Even some of the scouts who still have jobs complain that their opinions aren't valued as they once were, that bosses trust what their computers say over what the scouts tell them about a player.

The move to a reliance on big data has without doubt changed the game and led to changes in many of the unwritten rules. There will be more changes to come, because the available data keeps getting better and the analysis of it does, too.

But there's still plenty that the data doesn't show, and there are still things that are more evident when you watch a game in person than when you look at video. There are things you learn by talking to a player's teammates or to those who have coached or managed him.

Teams that come up with better information and better ways to use it will always have an edge.

The game changes. As Kapler said, we all need to be open to changing our minds.

3

Some Teams Get It

WHEN YOU ASK VETERAN MAJOR-LEAGUE PLAYERS WHERE they learned to play the game the right way, some mention a family member or a high school or college coach. Some mention a player they watched and respected as a kid, or a teammate that took time with them when they were young.

But quite a few of them will credit the organization that brought them to the big leagues. You hear it from players raised by the Yankees, by players raised by the Red Sox and the Twins, and just as often from players who came up with the Atlanta Braves over the last 30 years.

There was always a "Dodger way to play baseball," to quote the title of the 1954 book Al Campanis wrote when he was the team's scouting director, on the way to becoming general manager.

As Ross Newhan wrote in the *Los Angeles Times* in 2008, "the 'Dodger way' formed a significant part of the club's aura and attraction for decades, tutored to rookies in night classes at Dodgertown, envied and emulated by other organizations."

Newhan also asked whether the Dodgers under the Frank McCourt ownership of the early 2000s had lost their way.

"Was the book eventually misplaced?" he wrote. "Has it now been permanently lost?"

Organizations change over time, but many executives since Campanis have vowed to create an atmosphere that will also be envied and emulated. Some have even succeeded.

"There's a ton of accountability in that [Boston Red Sox] organization," said Travis Shaw, who was drafted by the Red Sox in 2011 and went through every level of the minor leagues with the Sox before coming to the big leagues in 2015. Shaw was traded to the Milwaukee Brewers after the 2016 season, but the lessons learned in the Red Sox organization stuck with him.

"It was play hard and don't take the name on the front of the uniform for granted," he said. "They always reminded you of the tradition, and that it was a privilege to put on that uniform."

When Shaw got to the major leagues, he found that Dustin Pedroia and David Ortiz policed the clubhouse the same way it was done in the minor leagues with the Red Sox. It was the same way for years with the Yankees, where Derek Jeter led the way, and also with the Braves with players like Chipper Jones, Brian McCann, and now Freddie Freeman.

It starts well before a player gets to the big leagues. Brian Butterfield played five years in the Yankees system and later returned to the organization as a coach and minor-league manager. Butterfield has gone on to work as a major-league coach with the Arizona Diamondbacks, Blue Jays, Red Sox, and Chicago Cubs, but he never forgot how things were with the Yankees.

"It all started back in the day with the short haircuts, and wearing your uniform a certain way," said Butterfield. "There were just certain things. It was cool because it made them different from just about every organization in baseball."

The Yankees still require players to cut their hair short, even in the major leagues. Other teams have had similar rules, at least in the minors.

When reliever Jason Motte signed with the Atlanta Braves in April 2017, he had to shave the beard he had worn for years, because he was going to pitch first in Triple-A and the Braves don't allow facial hair for their minor-league players.

Does any of that matter for winning? Butterfield thinks it does.

"No doubt," he said. "And I think it's been reflected through the years in the way the organization has approached things, the way they play the game. You'd always think the Yankees would come and play, kick your ass, and go home and go to bed. That's the way. It's a proud franchise. They've had a lot of good people leading the way, starting with George Steinbrenner."

It's not all about facial hair. The 2004 Red Sox famously called themselves "the Idiots." Johnny Damon had the beard and the long hair. As Kevin Millar said years later, "We were just the opposite of the Yankees."

The Yankees aren't alone, but they've been among the most successful in recent years at establishing a tradition of respect and watching their players carry it through. You never hear opposing players complain about the way Aaron Judge carries himself on the field or off it, just as you never heard anyone complain about Jeter.

Other organizations have been reminded how difficult it can be to maintain the tradition.

For years, the St. Louis Cardinals had a similar reputation. It went all the way back to Branch Rickey, the same man who once tutored Campanis in the "Dodger way." Rickey signed an infielder named George Kissell in 1940, and Kissell stayed with the Cardinals for almost 70 years and was responsible for what became known as the "Cardinal way."

"It's a cultural issue, I believe, and it's something we talk very much about," said Mike Matheny, who played five years in the major leagues with the Cardinals and later worked in the farm system before taking over as manager in 2012. "It's understanding not just respect for the game but respect for the organization and what the product should look like. That's been our aim, not necessarily to [win games] but to get to what looks like Cardinal baseball."

Matheny did speak often about the "Cardinal way" and "what looks like Cardinal baseball." In the end, though, he wasn't able to get his teams to follow through often enough, and just before the 2018 All-Star break the Cardinals fired him as manager.

The Cardinals made Mike Shildt the interim manager for the rest of 2018, and later gave him a full-time contract that runs through 2020. That may have come as a surprise to many who hadn't heard of him, but it fit with a desire to go back to what once made the Cardinals great. Shildt was a Kissell disciple, so much so that when Kissell's son Richard made copies of Kissell's notebook to give to those in the organization who were closest to him, Shildt was one of the recipients.

Shildt got his start in baseball as a clubhouse kid for the Baltimore Orioles' Double-A team in Charlotte, back when the "Orioles way" was as well-known as the "Dodger way" or the "Cardinals way."

"I got to see what that organization looked like, how it ran, so when I got to the Cardinals [in 2003] it was familiar," Shildt told Derrick Goold for a 2017 story in the *St. Louis Post-Dispatch*. "It was very fundamentals-based. There was an attention to details. There was an accountability. These things, ingrained in me then, made sense now. Continuity. Structures. A certain way you did things. My formative years were spent in a ballpark, in an organization that feels eerily similar at that time to the Cardinals. So, it's been in my blood."

The best organizations do feel similar in their approach to the game and to teaching the game's unwritten rules. Butterfield found that in going from the Yankees to the Red Sox. Shildt found it in coming to the Cardinals after growing up with the Orioles.

Any player fortunate enough to be raised in one of baseball's best organizations will know it, too.

4

Leave Your Ego at the Door

IN HIS HALL OF FAME INDUCTION SPEECH IN JULY 2018, ALAN
Trammell talked about what a difference Sparky Anderson made
when he took over as Detroit Tigers manager in 1979.

"Sparky's way was team first, always team first," Trammell
said. "Check your ego at the door."

A few minutes later, Trevor Hoffman walked to the microphone and said basically the same thing.

"I define chemistry as you leave your ego at the door, be
unselfish, trust one another, overcome odds, and always try to
find fun in the game," Hoffman said.

On almost any championship team, you'll hear players, managers, and coaches say some version of the same thing. And while
it has nothing to do with scoring a run or making a catch, you
could call it one of baseball's biggest unwritten rules.

Baseball is unusual among our team games, because so much
of the way the game is played is about a one-on-one confronta-
tion. Some of the best pitchers in history have had reputations

for being selfish, and the same has been said of some of the best hitters.

It's true there are times you want a hitter to give himself up or to think more about moving runners than trying to hit the ball out of the ballpark. Runner on second, nobody out, you'd like to see a ball to the right side that advances the runner to third where he can score on an out. Similarly, with that runner on third and less than two out, you want a ball put in play. A home run would be fine, but a strikeout that results from swinging for the fences is the perfect example of selfishness getting in the way of winning.

But if you're the best hitter in the lineup and there's a runner in scoring position, go ahead and expand your strike zone and try to drive him in. You'd be helping your team that way more than if you take a pitch just off the plate and take a walk that brings up a lesser hitter.

Anderson and other great managers talked about knowing the scoreboard. Down more than a run in the late innings, you have to understand your team needs baserunners more than anything. One-run game in the late innings, especially with two out, look for a pitch to drive out of the park if you're that kind of hitter (and in today's game, most are).

But even if some of those actions may seem selfish taken out of context, they're all based on giving the team the best chance of winning. The same goes for a reliever who tells his manager he doesn't need to be the closer.

When Andrew Miller came to the New York Yankees as a free agent in time for the 2015 season, he told them he'd pitch in any role that would help the team. That season, Yankees manager Joe Girardi used Miller as his closer, even though the lefty had never held that role in his first nine major-league seasons. When he came to the Yankees, Miller had just one save in 259 big-league appearances, most of them as a reliever.

Miller proved a successful closer, with 36 saves in 38 chances and a 2.04 ERA. But that December, the Yankees had a chance to acquire Aroldis Chapman at a bargain price from the Cincinnati Reds, because Chapman was facing a domestic violence charge.

The Yankees traded for Chapman, even though they already had a successful closer, because they understood what kind of teammate Miller was. He didn't complain at all about changing roles, picking up nine saves during the time Chapman was suspended or otherwise unavailable, and pitching very successfully in the eighth inning when Chapman had the glory (and save opportunity) in the ninth.

The Yankees traded both Chapman and Miller that July. Chapman went to the Chicago Cubs and helped them win their first World Series championship in 108 years. Miller went to the Cleveland Indians, where manager Terry Francona took advantage of his unselfishness and turned him into one of the best postseason bullpen weapons in baseball history.

Miller had just one save in 10 appearances in that postseason, but he was so dominant he was named Most Valuable Player in the American League Championship Series and nearly got the Indians their first World Series title in 68 years.

While managers like to have set roles and many relievers like to have an idea when they're going to be used, more than one manager has said, "Your role is to pitch when I put you in the game, and hopefully get outs."

When pitchers don't understand that, it can lead to trouble and sometimes it can lead to roster moves that might otherwise sound surprising.

At the July 31 trading deadline in 2018, the Washington Nationals sent reliever Brandon Kintzler to the Chicago Cubs. A day later, they designated reliever Shawn Kelley for assignment. General manager Mike Rizzo acknowledged to reporters that neither move was made because of how the guy pitched but rather because of how he acted. Kintzler and Kelley apparently weren't happy with how they were being used by manager Dave Martinez. The *Washington Post* reported the Nationals also believed Kintzler was the source for stories suggesting problems inside the clubhouse.

"If you're not in, you're in the way," Rizzo said, in a variation of the check-your-ego-at-the-door maxim.

The last straw with Kelley came when Martinez brought him in against the New York Mets with the Nationals leading 25–1. Kelley threw his glove while staring at Martinez after Kelley allowed a home run to Mets outfielder Austin Jackson. While Kelley insisted to reporters that he had only been frustrated with the umpires, it was clear to many in attendance that Martinez was the subject of his anger.

Rizzo saw it that way.

"I thought it was truly a day we should have been happy and celebrating—we had a big win against a division rival and felt good about ourselves," Rizzo told reporters "And such a selfish act is not what we're here for."

Kelley wasn't the first player to lose a job because he showed disrespect. Miguel Montero was a backup catcher for the Chicago Cubs, important enough that he appeared in four of the seven games in the 2016 World Series. By July of 2017, Montero was an ex-Cub, designated for assignment and traded to the Toronto Blue Jays soon after a late-June game against the Nationals.

The Nationals stole seven bases that night, but Montero wasn't sent packing because of an inability to throw anyone out. Instead, the problem was his postgame interview, when he put the blame on pitcher Jake Arrieta.

"That's the reason they were running left and right today," Montero told reporters. "It really sucked because the stolen bases go on me. But when you really look at it, the pitcher doesn't give me any time, so yeah, 'Miggy can't throw anyone out,' but my pitchers don't hold anyone on."

By the next morning, the Cubs designated Montero for assignment.

"Caught squealing," read the headline in the *Chicago Tribune*.

"[There are] too many young guys [in the clubhouse] who are impressionable," Cubs manager Joe Maddon explained to reporters. "With this young, impressionable group, to me, and a really good group that's going to be together for a long time, you don't want to foster, nurture, condone [Montero's] kind of message."

It didn't matter to the Cubs that Montero called Arrieta to apologize. The damage had been done and the Cubs were going to send the message that, as Mike Rizzo would say a year later, you're either in or you're in the way.

"When you point fingers, you're a selfish player," Cubs first baseman Anthony Rizzo said on WMVP radio.

Sometimes it doesn't even take pointing fingers. In 2011, pitcher Rafael Soriano angered the New York Yankees not because of anything he said but because of what he didn't say. Soriano was in his first month in New York and after a particularly bad performance (a four-run eighth inning that cost the Yankees a game), Soriano left without addressing the media.

Soriano wasn't the first or last player to leave without talking, but the Yankees quickly let him know that on their team, this was unacceptable. And their concern wasn't so much the reporters, but rather Soriano's teammates, who were put in the position of having to answer the questions that would properly have been directed at him. Reporters were left asking David Robertson, who followed Soriano into the game, and catcher Russell Martin about Soriano's poor performance.

The Yankees considered it a serious enough issue that both team president Randy Levine and general manager Brian Cashman phoned Scott Boras, the agent who represented Soriano. Boras then let Soriano know he had to be more accountable.

"He told me that whatever happened, that I've got to talk to you guys," Soriano told reporters the following day. "It doesn't have to be for a long time, but you guys have to hear from me."

It's part of being a good teammate, as Trammell and Hoffman both were when they played. It helped get them to the Hall of Fame.

5

As Adrian Beltre Proves, You Can Still Have Fun

SO MANY OF THE UNWRITTEN RULES COVER THINGS YOU can't do as a major-league player, or things that might get you in trouble with your teammates or your opponents. But the game is still supposed to be fun, and guys who make it fun can still find themselves on the way to join Trammell and Hoffman in Cooperstown.

Adrian Beltre proves that, although if you watch a tape of his first major-league hit, you'd never know it. Beltre was a 19-year-old kid back then, in 1998, and he smacked a Chuck Finley pitch into left field for a run-scoring double that night at Dodger Stadium. On the tape, you hear Vin Scully talking about the great numbers Beltre put together at Double-A San Antonio (.321, 13 home runs, in 64 games), about how Beltre was "a very aggressive hitter," and how "it didn't take long for him to collect his first base hit and RBI."

One other thing about that tape: as the camera shows Beltre standing at second base, the kid doesn't even crack a smile.

Smiling wasn't against baseball's rules, even then. Not the written rules, obviously, but not even the unwritten ones. But young players were still being schooled to avoid showing too much emotion. It's a long season. Don't get too high or too low. Never forget the game will humble you.

It still will, but thankfully it's now more than okay to show you're enjoying it when things are going well. And even sometimes when they're not. It took Beltre the better part of four seasons to feel comfortable showing emotion and being himself on the field, but he and the game have adjusted over a playing career that ended with his retirement announcement after the 2018 season.

"I don't think he's ever had a bad day at the ballpark," said Doug Brocail, a former major-league pitcher who was on the Texas Rangers' coaching staff in the latter years of Beltre's career. "He's ultra-fun. It's playful and fun, and it keeps guys from insanity."

Beltre provides proof that players today can win respect for "playing the game the right way" while also having fun doing it. As he neared the end of his career, it's possible no one was more respected, and also possible that no one had more fun.

Beltre almost danced in the batters box, asked umpires to check for help when he was sure he had checked his swing, and sometimes ran into the outfield or far onto the infield grass when he was caught in a rundown he knew he couldn't get out of. With the Rangers, he also collaborated with shortstop Elvis Andrus on a pantomime routine where both would set up at the same time to catch a pop fly.

"It's like the Harlem Globetrotters of baseball," said Dave Raymond, who chronicled it all as the Texas Rangers' television voice. "Half the time, I want our [producers] to roll out with 'Sweet Georgia Brown' going into the break. Adrian is Meadowlark Lemon, and Elvis is Curly Neal."

It was the Harlem Globetrotters and it wasn't, because as Beltre said, the Globetrotters' entire goal was to put on a show. He and Andrus were invested in winning games, but they were proving that you could do that and have fun at the same time.

"We have fun, and that's when we do the best," Andrus said. "We really have a passion for the game, and that's what attracted me to baseball in the first place: to be able to do something for hours and hours and still have fun with it. That's what I love about this game."

The key is to know how not to cross the line between enjoying yourself and becoming a clown, and it's possible no one has ever understood that line better than Beltre. A perfect example came in August 2018, in a game where Beltre and the Rangers faced the Seattle Mariners and Felix Hernandez, Beltre's former teammate and close friend.

In the second inning that night in Arlington, Texas, Hernandez struck out Beltre, who took an awkward swing for the third strike. Hernandez laughed as Beltre went to the dugout, and Beltre laughed right along with him.

Four innings later, Beltre hit Hernandez's first pitch for a home run to center field. But there were no laughs or other shows of emotion. Beltre put his head down and quietly circled the bases.

The reason was simple: Beltre's home run made the score 11–4 in the Rangers' favor. Hernandez had given up all 11 of those runs, in one of the worst starts of his career. Hernandez certainly would have understood if Beltre had celebrated—"Why didn't you do anything?" he texted Beltre after the game—but Beltre understood a celebration at that point could easily be taken the wrong way.

"Next time, if it's close, I will [do something]," Beltre said.

After 21 years in the major leagues, Beltre understood when a laugh could be helpful and also when it could be seen as showing someone up. The line can be a fine one at times, which is why Rangers general manager Jon Daniels jokingly says Beltre can be both the best and worst example for his younger players. While he's happy to have them joking around at the right time, they need to learn the line that Beltre never seems to cross.

"I always draw a line," Beltre said.

Andrus, in particular, had to learn. He eventually became the perfect foil for Beltre, not just when the two were going through their pop fly routine, but also when Andrus was going after Beltre during a celebration, trying to touch his head. Of all Beltre's quirks, one of the best known is that he never wants anyone touching his head.

"We're two grown men with a kid's soul," Andrus said.

He smiled when he said it. Beltre smiled plenty in the latter years of his career, although he sometimes first made a point of pretending to be angry with Andrus over something he claimed to find annoying. It was all part of what they did, enjoyable for them and entertaining for others.

It looked real, to the point friends asked Andrus why Beltre was mad at him and bloggers sometimes wrote that there was true anger. There wasn't.

"[Beltre] is never actually really mad at anyone," Rangers outfielder Joey Gallo said. "He's fake-mad a lot."

And nothing he did broke any of baseball's unwritten rules. That may not have been true two decades ago, back when Beltre broke into the game, but it's certainly true now.

Do it the right way, and it's absolutely alright to have fun playing the game.

6

When a Bat Flip Can Lead
to a Bloody Lip

THE PROBLEMS BEGIN WHEN A TEAM THINKS SOMEONE IS
having fun at their expense, or if what one team or player thinks
of as a legitimate celebration offends the group on the other side.
It can start with something as seemingly inoffensive as a bat flip.

Bat flips have been part of baseball for a while. With the help
of GIFs on Twitter and YouTube videos, they're more acceptable
than ever and more celebrated than ever. Many fans love them.
Many players do, too.

And many pitchers have come to accept them.

So why did Jose Bautista end up getting punched in the face?

It's a legit question. Bautista's bat flip in the 2015 playoffs was
epic, but it came after a huge home run. Bautista's Toronto Blue
Jays were tied 3–3 with the Texas Rangers in the winner-take-all
Game 5 of their American League Division Series. Bautista's three-
run home run off Sam Dyson changed the game and the series.

"I think that was a pretty big moment for the team and the
franchise," Bautista said in 2018. "I'm not trying to justify

anything, but if we want to talk about the moment, it's certainly an important one."

Bautista has never believed he did anything wrong that day, and I'm not sure he did. He definitely stood and watched the ball, which was clearly going out of the park. He dramatically flung the bat in the air. He may have turned his head a bit, but he didn't stare into the Rangers dugout, as some have charged.

Even so, the Rangers didn't like it. They didn't like losing, and they didn't like having to watch Bautista celebrate in a way they saw as shoving it in their face.

We know that because of what they said in the aftermath—"Jose needs to calm that down, just kind of respect the game a little more," Dyson told reporters after the game—but also because of what happened seven months later in Arlington, Texas.

It was the final game of a three-game series between the Jays and Rangers, the final game the two teams would play in the regular season in 2016 (although they would again meet in the Division Series, with the Jays winning in a much less dramatic three-game sweep). Bautista came to the plate leading off the eighth inning in that May 15 game, and Rangers reliever Matt Bush threw at him.

It was a first-pitch 95.7 mph fastball, according to MLB.com's Statcast, and it hit Bautista squarely on the left side. Bautista took his base with little delay, but the umpires quickly warned both teams that no further such pitches would be tolerated.

But that wasn't the end of it. Far from it.

When Blue Jays first baseman Justin Smoak hit a ground ball to third with one out in the inning, Bautista did more than just break up the double play. He went in late and hard on Rangers second baseman Rougned Odor in a clear response to getting hit by the pitch from Bush. Odor responded with a fist to Bautista's jaw, an image that was quickly shared around the baseball world.

The Rangers, it was said, finally had their revenge for the bat flip.

But why was revenge even needed? Did Bautista violate any of baseball's unwritten rules, the way those rules are accepted in the modern game?

The Rangers obviously thought so. They weren't alone.

"I know Odor gained a ton of respect in baseball [by punching Bautista]," said Ian Kinsler, the former Rangers second baseman, who was already gone from the team before both the flip and the fight. "He stood up for his team. In their eyes, [Bautista] was disrespectful."

Bautista will always maintain there was no disrespect, and he bristles at the suggestion that his celebration was in anyway premeditated.

"I don't think you plan that," he said. "I don't think there's a script, and I don't think you have time to figure out what you're going to do. It just kind of happens, and that's it. Would somebody apologize for making a diving play? It's an instinctual moment."

In contrast, the Rangers' response did seem planned, at least the part with him getting hit by the Matt Bush pitch. They chose to wait until his final at-bat in their final regular-season meeting, with a hard-throwing reliever on the mound.

"Pretty cowardly," Bautista told reporters that day. "It shows a little bit more of their colors."

It's not clear, though, that Bautista would have been any happier had the Rangers thrown at him in the first inning of their first 2016 meeting.

"Who cares now?" he said in 2018. "It's in the past."

The issue, though, is still very real today. In an era where bat flips have become more common and more accepted than ever, when are they considered okay and when are they not? And does it matter if the flip is more or less dramatic?

"In the playoffs and a late inning go ahead HR, there is nothing wrong with what @JoeyBats19 did," former Blue Jays star Joe Carter tweeted after Bautista's October flip. "In the regular season it's a nae nae."

It's an interesting distinction, one that Houston Astros shortstop Carlos Correa has made as well.

Correa flipped his bat after hitting a big home run for Puerto Rico in the 2017 World Baseball Classic, and again after his Game 3 home run in the 2017 World Series. But he said he would never flip his bat after a regular-season home run.

Still, everyone agrees there's no unwritten rule that says bat flips are reserved for October (or March in World Baseball Classic years) only. There is more of an understanding that it's best to reserve them for dramatic home runs, walkoffs, or other game-winners and the like.

But even that is flexible, in an era where some guys flip their bats after singles or sometimes even after walks.

Bautista is hardly a serial flipper, but a year almost to the day after the Odor punch that resulted from his flip flap, he again flipped his bat after an eighth-inning home run. Except this one was on a May night in Atlanta, and it came after a solo home run in a game the Blue Jays trailed 8–3. There had been a benches-clearing incident an inning earlier, but it hadn't directly involved Bautista.

Like the Rangers in 2015, the Braves didn't like the flip. The difference this time was that Bautista agreed with them, even as he was rounding the bases. He quickly understood the emotions of the moment, in a series where the Braves were already upset about losing their star first baseman, Freddie Freeman, to a broken wrist suffered when he was unintentionally hit by a pitch from Toronto's Aaron Loup.

"It wasn't a good moment to do anything like that," Bautista said in 2018. "I realized at the moment they had good reason to take offense."

The tape of the home run shows Bautista exchanging words with Braves catcher Kurt Suzuki as he crossed home plate, and the benches emptying after that. But Bautista said the words he said to Suzuki weren't angry ones.

"I took the time to let them know I didn't mean anything by it," he said.

That makes sense. Bautista obviously didn't want a fight. As the benches were emptying—the players in the dugout had no way to know Bautista had already apologized—Bautista headed to the Blue Jays dugout.

His apology either never reached or didn't satisfy Braves pitcher Eric O'Flaherty, who allowed the home run.

"That's something that's making the game tough to watch lately," O'Flaherty told reporters after the game. "It's just turned into look-at-me stuff; it's not even about winning anymore. Guy wants to hit a home run in a five-run game, pimp it, throw the bat around—I mean, I don't know. It's frustrating as a pitcher. I didn't see it at the time, but I saw the video—he looked at me, tried to make eye contact. It's just tired. We've seen it from him, though."

O'Flaherty couldn't resist a parting shot.

"I'm surprised he's ready to fight again after last year [with Odor]," he said.

This time, though, there would be no punch to the jaw.

7

Here's Some Flipping History

JOSE BAUTISTA DIDN'T INVENT THE BAT FLIP. NEITHER DID Yasiel Puig or Odubel Herrera or anyone else who was still playing Major League Baseball in 2018. That much we know.

We also know Bobby Thomson didn't flip his bat on the "Shot Heard 'Round the World" in 1951, and that Mickey Mantle didn't flip when he walked off the Cardinals in the 1964 World Series (well before anyone called it a walkoff). We know Kirk Gibson didn't flip when he homered off Rich Gossage in the 1984 World Series, or when he homered off Dennis Eckersley four Octobers later.

But Tom Lawless did.

Yeah, Tom Lawless, a guy who played eight years in the big leagues and hit two regular season home runs. Tom Lawless.

He homered off Frank Viola in Game 4 of the 1987 World Series, and after 10 steps down the first-base line, he flipped his bat. Flipped it good, too, high in the air.

"Look at this!" Tim McCarver said on TV as ABC showed the replay.

"I didn't remember flipping it," Lawless told reporters after the game. "I've never been in a position like this before."

"When he hit it and stood there, I thought it must be in the upper deck," Cardinals manager Whitey Herzog said. "It was about a foot out. I asked him about it later and he said he hit it as good as he could hit a ball. I said you better run."

When Lawless appeared as a guest during a 2017 Cardinals telecast, Dan McLaughlin asked him, "So are you the original bat flip guy?"

"Nooo," Lawless said. "Reggie Jackson had to do it before I did."

"Not like that," McLaughlin said.

"No," Lawless agreed. "Not like that. I don't have any idea why I did it. It just happened."

Reggie did flip his bat at times, but not like that. His flips, even on the biggest home runs, would hardly be seen as flips today. Even when he homered three times in a World Series game, he tossed the bat aside instead of really flipping it. It didn't go over his shoulder. It went past his feet.

The Lawless one, without doubt, was a flip.

Whether or not it started a trend, the fact is flipping would eventually become more widespread and unwritten rules about it would need to be established. How opponents would react to a flip might vary from pitcher to pitcher and team to team, but it would also depend on the flipper and the situation he flipped in. Do it in a World Series, as Lawless did, and you had a better chance of getting away without a fastball to the ribs the next time up. Do it when you're an established star, a big slugger like Barry Bonds, and you've got a good chance of getting away with it.

Do it in the middle of May when you're a rookie and you risk a reaction like Jimmy Rollins got in 2001. Rollins hit a home run off Steve Kline. He may or may not have really flipped. His manager, Larry Bowa, said, "he dropped it from his waist. Jimmy didn't do anything wrong that you don't see on *SportsCenter* every night."

What matters most, though, is the guy you might be showing up. Kline felt shown up and didn't appreciate it.

"You don't do that," he told reporters. "That's Little League stuff. I'll flip his helmet the next time. If Scott Rolen or Barry Bonds do it, it's no big deal. But not a first-year player."

Soon enough, though, bat flips were being celebrated.

By 2003, the Mariners did a television ad showing Bret Boone flipping his bat, and then flipping a rake while working in his yard, a spoon while eating, his toothbrush after brushing, and a phone after hanging up. YouTube came into being two years later, and before long flips could be shared around the world. Bat flip aficionados began watching their favorite flips from Korean baseball.

Is it any wonder more and more kids came to the big leagues as flippers?

Not all of them, though.

Aaron Judge doesn't flip. He didn't even do it when he hit his 49th and 50th home runs of the 2017 season, tying and eclipsing Mark McGwire's record for a major-league rookie. Judge calmly put the bat down and quickly began his trip around the bases.

Kris Bryant doesn't flip, either.

The Cubs star, who was the National League's Most Valuable Player in 2016, said he doesn't want to be the guy who flips his bat and then realizes it wasn't a home run after all. Bryant feels a long home run is enough of an embarrassment for the pitcher who serves it up, so there's no need for him to add to it.

Beyond that, though, Bryant said it's just not in his personality to add the extra flair of a bat flip to his game.

"I've never been that way, and I'm not going to be someone I'm not," Bryant said. "It's my personality. I get it, big situations, big home runs, far home runs, it's nice to sit there and admire what you just did. I've always thought that the insult is you've already hit the home run off the pitcher. That's plenty enough, for me. That's just who I've been my whole life."

Maybe Tom Lawless is always going to be that guy who flipped his bat in the 1987 World Series. But for the record, Frank Viola never did retaliate for Lawless' flip. He faced Lawless again two years later, when Lawless was playing for the Blue Jays, and Lawless struck out and grounded out in two at-bats.

8

If Baseball Is "Tired," Shouldn't It Be Okay to Show Some Emotion?

IN THE SPRING OF 2016, WASHINGTON NATIONALS STAR Bryce Harper did an interview with Tim Keown of *ESPN The Magazine*.

This was the interview where Harper called baseball "a tired sport." Plenty of people focused on that, and many who don't like Harper saw it as confirmation of their beliefs. In truth, Harper loves the game and its history. He wants the game to become more popular, especially among people in his age group. (Harper was 23 years old when the story came out.)

"I'm not saying baseball is, you know, boring or anything like that," Harper told Keown. But he also listed players who he considered fun: Matt Harvey, Jacob deGrom, Manny Machado, Joc Pederson, Andrew McCutchen, Yasiel Puig, and Jose Fernandez.

He singled out Fernandez, the Miami Marlins pitcher who would die in a boating accident late in the 2016 season.

"Jose Fernandez is a great example," Harper said. "Jose Fernandez will strike you out and stare you down into the dugout and pump his fist. And if you hit a homer and pimp it? He doesn't care. Because you got him. That's part of the game. It's not the old feeling—hoorah… if you pimp a homer, I'm going to hit you right in the teeth. No. If a guy pimps a homer for a game-winning shot… I mean—sorry."

Mike Matheny is 22 years older than Harper, enough that he's from a different generation of players. Matheny had been retired as a player for 10 years and was managing the St. Louis Cardinals when the Harper interview came out.

"Wow, times have changed since Bob Gibson, right?" Matheny said. "But if that's what they believe and that's what they're good with, I want to make sure I don't get stuck in what I think is right. I want to represent the team and what they think."

When Matheny took over as the Cardinals manager in 2012, he said he saw things from opponents that would have bothered him if he were behind the plate catching. As a catcher, he paid special attention to what the other team's hitters did, in part because he felt the need to defend his own pitcher. He wanted to defuse the situation before it got to the point where his pitcher might do something that got him in trouble.

As a manager, though, Matheny would see something that concerned him, then look down the dugout and see that his own players weren't offended by it.

"I mean there's stuff guys are doing now that players have just become okay with," Matheny said in 2017. "To me, it was my job as a catcher to defend a pitcher who might be getting shown up by a celebration. If I had to take over, that was something I'd been taught, so I was always hypersensitive to what was going on.

"But in my conversations with guys [as a manager], I'll ask, 'Does that bother you?' I get a lot of 'No, not really.'"

Eventually, Matheny's old-school attitudes may have helped lead to his downfall as a manager. Just before the All-Star break in 2018, the Cardinals fired Matheny, with president of baseball operations John Mozeliak saying the team wanted to "change the way we look at things."

The Cardinals were just 47–46 at the time of the move, and their 7½-game deficit in the National League Central no doubt had more to do with Matheny losing his job. But there was no question Matheny was also uncomfortable with some of the things he was seeing in baseball, and not just at the major-league level.

"I'm watching kids in youth baseball flip their bat and do cartwheels," he said.

Matheny hit 67 home runs in his big-league career and never flipped his bat.

"I never did anything worth flipping," he said.

Nice line, but in today's game you'll see players flip a bat after a single or even after a walk. The bigger point is that most of those flips don't offend the pitcher or anyone on the opposing team.

In the end, it's the players who decide what celebrations are acceptable and which ones aren't. In this era, it may not be true that anything goes, but it's close to that.

It's also true that you'd better be careful about taking offense at what a guy on the other team does, because there's a good chance someone on your team could do the exact same thing later on.

"You just have to look the other way," said Juan Samuel, a longtime major-league player who spent time as a coach and manager after he retired. "This is how it is today. You look down at the dugout and nobody's reacting to anything, so why am I going to?"

9

You Can Earn the Right
to Celebrate

NOT ALL CELEBRATIONS ARE CREATED EQUAL.

If it's a big enough moment, a guy can flip his bat high in the air. He can dance around the bases the way Kirk Gibson did in the 1988 World Series.

Everyone understood, including the pitcher who gave up one of the most famous home runs in World Series history.

"That's the ultimate time to have emotion," Dennis Eckersley told Gibson, in a joint interview they did on the Red Sox's NESN cable network in June 2018. "You're so glad and I'm so sad."

The moment matters. So does the guy doing the celebrating.

Eckersley got away with plenty of dramatic celebrations himself, when he was the best closer in the game. He would pump his fist after a strikeout. He would point.

As long as he kept it about himself and his own emotions, opponents mostly accepted it as just who Eck was and what he did. Even he could sometimes go too far, as he did in the 1992 playoffs when he stared into the Toronto Blue Jays dugout after a big strikeout.

"Little League," Jack Morris called it that day. And when the Jays tied the game on Roberto Alomar's ninth-inning home run off Eckersley and went on to win it, taking a three games to one lead in the series, they let Eckersley know what they thought.

"Old Eck stuck it in our face and gave us reason to be happy as hell when we came back," Morris said. "You let sleeping giants lie. The poor guy wouldn't look over [after Alomar's homer] like he did when he struck the guy out."

"They got the payback, right?" Eckersley responded. "They can gloat in that, while I eat crow."

He was willing to eat crow, and he was also willing to accept it when a hitter like Gibson celebrated a huge moment. Big moments by big hitters make a little more drama acceptable.

David Ortiz could stand and stare when he hit a big home run. So could Barry Bonds or Ken Griffey Jr.

It's the guy who hits five home runs a year and wants to flip a bat. That's what gets to pitchers. It's the guy who flips his bat after a single.

"I don't think Aaron Judge is going to stand there and watch, which is ultimately why I love him," Astros pitcher Gerrit Cole said. "But one of the most iconic [scenes] is Manny [Ramirez] standing there with his hands over his head. There are guys that have been around for a long time. When you have 600 home runs and you want to stop and look at it, I sure as hell am not going to tell you otherwise. That's your own deal.

"But there are only a few guys who have that many home runs, and you might not know that by watching [the games]."

Cole is right about Judge, who hit a major-league rookie record 52 home runs in 2017 with the Yankees. He didn't flip his bat after any of them, and didn't take his time running around the bases, either.

Judge told Kevin Kernan of the *New York Post* that he'll never stop and watch, because one time when he was a senior in high school, he stood and watched a ball that hit the top of the fence.

"I didn't even make it to second base," Judge said. "After that moment I said it would be the last time I don't hustle."

Plenty of players come to the major leagues without learning the same lesson. When Jose Ramirez was a young player with the Indians in 2015, the Twins got upset when he took too long to round the bases after a home run against them—taking nearly eight seconds just to get to first base. And that was after he flipped his bat. The Twins let him know they didn't approve, and even Ramirez's own manager said something.

"Good swing, poor judgment," Terry Francona told reporters that day. "He'll learn. Hopefully not the hard way, but he'll learn."

It seems he did. In the years since 2015, Ramirez has become one of baseball's big stars, the type of guy who might get away with admiring his home runs. But of the 29 homers he hit in the 2017 season, he never took even 24 seconds to circle the bases.

Even in 2015, Ramirez was fortunate. There was a time when the Twins' disapproval would have resulted in a fastball to the ribs. They never did throw at Ramirez.

Carlos Gomez wasn't so fortunate. Gomez hit a walkoff home run against the Twins in April 2018. He flipped his bat. He threw his arms in the air. He wagged his tongue. And he took his time rounding the bases. Statcast timed his trot at 28.85 seconds, incredibly slow for a guy who is fast.

"I was not trying to disrespect anybody," Gomez told the *Tampa Bay Times* the next day.

But when the Rays went to Minnesota three months later, Twins pitcher Jose Berrios greeted Gomez with a 90.9 mph fastball on the hip.

Gomez won't get anywhere close to 600 home runs in his career (he had 142 in 12 seasons through 2018), but he won't make any apologies for playing the game with some flair.

"It's something I know a lot of people are talking good about this, that baseball needs more of that," Gomez told the *Times*. "And some people say it's not good. If enjoying and having fun in baseball is bad, I'm guilty."

David Ortiz didn't hit 600 home runs, but he did hit 541 in his 20-year career. And after many of them, he took his time rounding the bases. From 2010 to '16, a guy named Larry Granillo timed home run trots and posted them at a website he called tatertrottracker.com. In 2013, by Granillo's calculations, Ortiz had seven of the 10 slowest trots. Twelve times in the seven seasons Granillo timed the trots, Ortiz took more than 30 seconds to get around the bases.

No one minded. It was David Ortiz.

Now MLB.com's Statcast is able to time every trot electronically. Nelson Cruz had the longest one of 2017, at 33.37 seconds, not counting trots interrupted by injury or ones where the batter had to wait to see if a ball would be called fair or foul. But there were four other guys who had at least one trot of at least 31 seconds in 2017 (Anthony Rizzo, Yasiel Puig, Hanley Ramirez, and Manny Machado).

Puig needed 32.1 seconds to make it around the bases after a home run against the Mets that June.

Mets players Yoenis Cespedes and Jose Reyes let him know between innings that he might not want to do it again. Puig is not normally a slow guy, but his trot that day was one of the slowest of the entire season.

"[Cespedes] told me, 'Try to run a little faster,'" Puig told reporters after the game.

In today's game, some pitchers will tell you they don't mind what a hitter does. But if gaining respect from everyone matters to you, you don't take 32.1 seconds to circle the bases and you don't pimp a single in the middle of a nothing game in August.

"Sometimes I feel people are over-glorifying themselves," Cole said. "You know, it's like, dude, you hit a single. It takes two more hits to score you. It takes someone else to drive you in."

10

The Puig Way to Play Baseball

BEFORE THE DODGERS GAVE YASIEL PUIG $42 MILLION AND signed him to his first professional contract, they had never watched him play in a game in person. They didn't even see him run or throw in a private workout in Mexico.

Puig had played two seasons in Cuba's highest league, but those games are off-limits to scouts from major-league teams. The Dodgers had only seen a YouTube clip of Puig making a diving catch and throwing the ball back to the infield.

Other Cuban stars had been exposed to the baseball world in international tournaments. Cuban officials rarely put Puig on the roster to travel to events off the island, rightly fearing he would be a strong candidate to defect. Puig reportedly made 13 attempts to leave Cuba before he was finally successful in getting to Mexico.

"He wasn't in baseball shape," said Logan White, who led the Dodger contingent in Mexico as the team's vice president of amateur scouting. "He'd take a swing and gasp for air. But I knew I hadn't seen an athlete like that."

He was absolutely an athlete—Dodgers Rookie League manager Matt Martin compared Puig to football star Adrian Peterson before he'd even seen him play in a game—but there was no way he was going to have a feel for the unwritten rules of the game as it is played in the United States. No one should have expected that, especially with the limited time he spent in the minor leagues.

Puig signed with the Dodgers on June 29, 2012. He played his first minor-league game five weeks later in the Arizona Rookie League. He came to the big leagues on June 3, 2013, not even a year after that workout in Mexico.

"I needed to learn about everything," Puig said. "I learned to play baseball slower, and as a teammate, everybody playing today, to win. There's only 90 games or so in the season in Cuba. Here there's 162. You fly across the country."

Puig had never seen crowds in Cuba like he saw every night at Dodger Stadium, where 37,055 showed up for his debut on a Monday night, and where the Dodgers averaged more than 46,000 a game for the season.

"I want to give back to the community in Los Angeles, because every day and every minute the stadium is full," he said. "And that's the way I like it. That's the fun of baseball."

By the late summer and early fall of 2018, Puig was giving back to LA in the best way possible, with home runs that mattered in games the Dodgers had to win, and with home run celebrations that could get everyone involved. He homered twice in one crucial game against the St. Louis Cardinals, three times the next day as the Dodgers beat the Cardinals again.

And when he hit a tie-breaking, three-run, pinch-hit home run a few days later in a huge game against the Colorado Rockies, the Puig celebration may have broken some hearts in the Rocky Mountains but broke no baseball rules, written or unwritten.

As Andy McCullough described it in the next morning's *Los Angeles Times*, Puig "was an engine of perpetual motion.

"He pointed to his teammates while rounding first base. He asked the group to show him the money. He flexed his biceps. He pounded his chest. He implored the crowd to scream louder and louder before he disappeared into a blur of Dodgers, waiting out a kiss from hitting coach Turner Ward to commemorate the homer."

Puig had always wanted to show the fans how he felt, but he came to realize that some of the expressions of emotion didn't go over the same way they would have back home, unless they came at the right time. The game has become much more accepting of open shows of emotion, but Puig has also gained a better understanding of what will be accepted and what could cause friction.

"In Cuba, it's like in the Dominican or Puerto Rico," he said. "All the Latin countries, we play with fun, play with love, sometimes play a little bit hard. We might do things like a bat flip. In those countries, it's not considered so bad, but here, the other team might think it doesn't show respect for the game."

Learning all that wasn't easy for Puig. In December 2015, two and a half years after Puig's big-league debut, Scott Miller wrote a piece for Bleacher Report headlined: "Is There Anybody Left in Los Angeles Whom Yasiel Puig Hasn't Alienated?"

"He is the worst person I have ever seen in this game," one ex-Dodger told Miller. "Ever."

Puig still didn't know how to act on the field. He didn't know how to act off the field, or with his teammates. He ran into outs on the bases. He ran late and often didn't make it to the clubhouse on time. He fought with teammates.

The following summer, after first trying unsuccessfully to trade Puig, the Dodgers sent him to the minor leagues for what turned out to be a month-long stay.

Eventually, he began to learn what playing in the major leagues—and what being a major leaguer—was all about.

The game's unwritten rules were no longer such a mystery to him. Puig became a more popular figure in the clubhouse and an everyday player on the field, as the Dodgers went all the way to Game 7 of the World Series in 2017, before losing to the Astros.

During that postseason of 2017, Miller wrote another Bleacher Report column. The headline on this one: "Puig Being Puig Is Back: Bat Flips, Tongue Wags Turn Problem Child to Catalyst."

"He's the best," Dodgers pitcher Alex Wood told Miller. "He does some dumb things sometimes, but we love him."

And when Carlos Correa of the Astros executed a pretty nice bat flip after a huge home run in Game 2 of the World Series, it was Puig himself who was asked to judge whether Correa had bent or broken any unwritten rule.

"He was happy, and that's the way you should play in the World Series," Puig said that night. "He wasn't batting too well, he was only getting a few hits, and when he hit the home run, it was a moment for him to be happy. I'm glad he was able to celebrate that way."

By 2018, when Puig had played more than 600 major-league games and had a better feel for American culture, he had changed the way he played. He wanted to fit in, and he was learning exactly what that meant.

He could still find himself in the middle of controversy, as he did that August in a game against the rival San Francisco Giants. Puig fouled off a pitch from Giants reliever Tony Watson, then grabbed his bat by the barrel in frustration. In his mind, he was showing natural emotion at missing what he felt might be the best pitch he'd see from Watson in that at-bat.

But Giants catcher Nick Hundley took exception and had words for Puig, apparently believing Puig was showing up Watson. Before long, they were shoving and the benches were emptying, and one more time Puig was having to explain himself to reporters.

"[Hundley] told me to stop complaining and get back into the box, and when I got into his face he told me to also get out of his face, so that's when I got upset," Puig said. "I didn't like that he was telling me what to do, and then he said some words to me in English that I really can't repeat, that's why I was upset."

Reaction to the incident showed how Puig's image has changed—many defended him and blamed Hundley, and Dodger Stadium fans cheered him loudly—but also how it hasn't. He may never escape the role of lightning rod, and he may never convince everyone he can do more good than bad.

In the wake of the battle with Hundley, *Los Angeles Times* columnist Bill Plaschke lit into Puig, calling him "senseless and reckless in allowing Hundley to bait him into a fight" and suggesting the Dodgers should "trade him for a reliever."

Even Dodgers manager Dave Roberts told reporters he would talk to Puig about controlling his emotions and understanding he needs to avoid getting ejected from games.

"Do I wish he could have stayed in the game? Absolutely," Roberts said. "He's more valuable in the game than out of the game."

He was out of the rest of that game against the Giants, which the Dodgers went on to lose. He was also suspended for two more games by MLB, and the Dodgers split those two against the New York Mets.

When he came back from the suspension, Puig homered seven times in his next 35 at-bats. As the Dodgers were taking control in the National League West, he was one of the biggest factors—and certainly one of the most demonstrative.

It was #Puigtember, as Dodgers closer Kenley Jansen dubbed it on Twitter.

Puig has changed. He hasn't changed completely. He doesn't want to, and he shouldn't want to.

"If I hit a home run, I'll still flip my bat because it's in the moment," he said. "Something exciting is coming into my body. I don't mean to disrespect the pitcher or the other team, but it's something exciting."

No kid raised on the American way to play baseball could have said it any better.

11

Loving the Game the Latin Way

ON A TUESDAY NIGHT IN MARCH 2013, A GROUP OF THE best baseball players from the Dominican Republic stepped on a baseball field in San Francisco and proved they could win a world championship playing the game their own way.

They could dance and they could chirp, and they could even carry a lucky plantain with them wherever they went. Team Dominican Republic won the World Baseball Classic (WBC) that night at AT&T Park, beating Team Puerto Rico in the final game and showing the baseball world that flair and emotion and fun can go right along with talent on the road to winning.

"I hope people in the U.S. understand the way we play baseball," Octavio Dotel said on the field that night, after he and his teammates celebrated by carrying a huge Dominican Republic flag from the mound out to center field. "This is how we play the game. We love this game. We have it in our heart. That's why we can't hold it in."

For years, they were told they had to hold it in, that the style they played with at home and in the winter leagues wouldn't translate to the major leagues or to a 162-game season. Don't get too high, don't get too low, and by all means don't do anything that might cause anyone else to take offense.

In another era, that could even include speaking their own language in the clubhouse. When Hall of Fame first baseman Orlando Cepeda wrote his book, *Baby Bull: From Hardball to Hard Time and Back*, he included a story about Alvin Dark taking over as the San Francisco Giants manager in the spring of 1961.

The Giants of that era featured more players born in Latin America than any other team, and the group included not just Cepeda (who would finish second in Most Valuable Player voting that season), but also Hall of Fame pitcher Juan Marichal and two of the three Alou brothers, Felipe and Matty (Jesus was still in the minor leagues and would join his brothers with the Giants two years later).

Dark, who was raised in segregation-era Louisiana and debuted as a major-league player a year before Jackie Robinson broke the color line, called the group together behind second base and delivered a message that even in that very different era shocked the players he was addressing.

Some of their teammates, Dark claimed, had complained that the players from Latin America were speaking Spanish in the clubhouse and those players couldn't understand what they were saying. Dark's solution: no Spanish in the clubhouse.

"Alvin, I won't do that," Cepeda responded. "I'm Puerto Rican, others are Dominican, and I'm proud of what I am. This is a disgrace to my race."

Later on, Cepeda wrote, Dark also banned Latin music from his Giants clubhouse.

You can imagine how he would have felt about a pitcher dancing on the mound, as Pedro Strop had done in that 2013 WBC final. Or a pitcher punctuating a save by firing an imaginary arrow into the night, as Fernando Rodney did that night and also after many of his 300-plus saves in the major leagues.

Or an American-born kid named Marcus Stroman doing a shoulder-shake as he strutted off the mound four years later, the night Team USA joined the fun and won the 2017 WBC.

A half-century after Dark issued his no-Spanish edict, the language is heard every day in every clubhouse in the major leagues. Japanese, Korean, and Chinese players have become big-league regulars, too, but the numbers and the style of the players from Latin America have had the biggest impact.

A major-league game today still doesn't look like a winter league game in Santo Domingo or even like a WBC game featuring the Dominican Republic, Puerto Rico, or Venezuela.

"Trust me, the showboating in winter ball is on a different level," said Jose Mota, a Dominican-born announcer whose father Manny played 20 seasons in the major leagues.

But in terms of style, flair, and out-and-out emotion, baseball in the major leagues now doesn't look anything like the game Cepeda and others were asked to play in the 1960s, either. It doesn't look like the game Juan Samuel found when he left the Dominican Republic to sign with the Philadelphia Phillies in 1980.

"For me, coming over here, it was just paying attention to what other guys were doing," Samuel said. "I didn't see any of that, bat-flipping or whatever. You had a few guys that were doing things here and there, but I didn't see much. You had a few guys who might flip their helmet when they were running."

Even at home, Samuel hadn't been as demonstrative as others, but he quickly learned that added flair might be frowned upon here.

"I didn't want to draw any negative attention to myself," he said. "I was going to [get attention] by playing as hard as I can, taking the extra base. If someone in the outfield took too long to get the ball in, then I'm going to take the extra base and embarrass you that way, but not the other way."

It worked for Samuel, who played 16 years in the major leagues and went on to coach and manage. But as he points out, he really didn't have much choice.

"We didn't have a lot of Latinos on the team when I started," he said.

Samuel's first full year in the big leagues was with the 1984 Phillies, who had a few players from Puerto Rico but no others besides Samuel from the Dominican Republic.

"I think that helped me [adapt]," he said. "Because when you see more guys [from the same country] together, they start acting more like guys from back home."

Years later, Samuel was a coach for the Dominican Republic team that won the WBC.

"This is the biggest win our country has ever had," he said when Team DR won the title.

It was, but it was also a big night for baseball, a night to remember how having fun and celebrating in your own way can still fit in with winning.

"You see major-league stars acting like kids," said Team DR general manager Moises Alou (Felipe's son).

As I wrote that night on CBSSports.com, what's wrong with that?

12

There Will Always Be Some Culture Clashes

THERE'S NO DOUBT BASEBALL HAS GAINED FROM THE influx of players from Latin America, both in terms of the talent coming into the game and the emotions and excitement those players have brought with them. Even if they can't play the exact same way in the majors as they play at home or in the WBC, many of them have helped bring a flair to the game.

It's still not easy. You don't hear it as much as you once did, but every now and then someone whispers that a team isn't winning because it has "too many Latins." Philadelphia Phillies Hall of Famer Mike Schmidt had to apologize to Phillies outfielder Odubel Herrera in 2017 because Schmidt had said the Phillies couldn't build their team around a player who wasn't fluent in English.

"I think he can't be a guy that would sort of sit in a circle with four, five American players and talk about the game; or try and learn about the game or discuss the inner workings of the game;

or come over to a guy and say, 'Man, you gotta run that ball out,'"
Schmidt had said in an interview on WIP radio.

As then-Phillies manager Pete Mackanin told reporters that
day, "It was an ill-advised comment."

Teams are doing a better job of making sure players they
sign get instruction in English and help with American culture.
Two of the young stars who came to the major leagues in 2018—
Dominican-born Juan Soto of the Washington Nationals (19 years
old) and Venezuelan-born Gleyber Torres of the Yankees
(21 years old)—were fluent to the point of being able to do radio
and television interviews in English.

More American players, coaches, and managers are learning
Spanish, too, and teams understand the importance of having
Latin American coaches on their staff.

But the way players from Latin America are scouted and
signed presents other issues. While players from the United
States, Canada, and Puerto Rico are subject to a draft and aren't
normally eligible to be picked until the year their class graduates
from high school, players from other countries in the Americas
can sign as long as they will turn 17 by the end of the first season
of their contract (in effect, if they are within two months of their
16th birthday when the signing period begins each year on July 2).

To be seen by scouts and have a chance at the big bonuses
that go to the best prospects, players who are much younger than
16 go to camps and prioritize baseball over education. And with
the difficult economic situation in some of those countries, kids
and their families bet that concentrating on baseball can lead to
a contract that could provide life-changing money.

"They're recruiting young kids from 12 [years old]," complained Martin Prado, who was 17 when he signed with the Atlanta Braves out of Venezuela in 2001. "By the time I started thinking about playing professionally, I was already 15 or 16. Now, 11 years old, they're already in an academy [for baseball], because when they get to 15, they have to be ready for July 2."

For those that make it, everything can be great. Even with new rules that have limited the money teams can spend on international signings, there were at least 20 players in 2018 alone that signed for $1 million or more out of the Dominican Republic, Venezuela, or Colombia, according to MLB.com.

But what about the kids who don't get big money and never make it, or the kids who don't end up good enough to get a contract at all?

"Just think about all the time you have to sacrifice," Prado said. "So education is not a priority. Unfortunately, it is [too bad]."

Prado feels blessed he was able to stay in school as long as he did. He also feels blessed that he was good enough to play for 13 seasons in the major leagues, through 2018. While he was never one of the game's biggest stars, the amount of money in professional baseball meant he had earned more than $77 million in his career.

Prado also felt fortunate to sign with the Atlanta Braves, and to come up in an organization that taught him about American baseball.

"They taught me how to play the game right and respect the game," he said. "As much as this game gives you, it can take it away. It looks cool to celebrate success, but my message [to younger players] is I hope you celebrate when you struggle, too. I had a hitting coach in rookie ball who played 11 years in the big leagues. His name is Sixto Lezcano. He came up to me one day, out of nowhere, and told me if you ever make it to the big leagues, make sure you buy a big bed, like a mattress."

"A mattress?" Prado asked.

"Yeah, just get a big one, a cozy one," Lezcano told him. "So when you fall from way up there, you don't hit yourself too hard on the way down."

Prado wasn't a flashy player by today's standards. But he liked to celebrate his success a little, as he puts it. And when he was in the big leagues and he eventually and inevitably had a year when things didn't go as well, he understood exactly what Lezcano had been trying to tell him all those years before.

He tries to pass that message on.

"I don't think they listen," he said with a chuckle. "But to be honest, baseball has given me so much, for me and my family, that the least I can do is give young kids advice so they don't make the same mistakes I made in the past."

And when Prado talks about the major-league players he respects, he cites the same players an old-school scout might mention.

Buster Posey, he said. Or Kris Bryant.

"Former MVP," he said. "Just hit the ball and run. There's a few guys. They look so much better as a star. You see a guy who is a five-tool guy, but it's even better when they do everything right. It's more of an impact for me."

Prado was so taken with what he was taught in the Braves organization that he said he even applied it to his life away from baseball, to what he would teach his daughters.

"Respect," he said. "And they have to earn my respect."

And that's a sentiment that should mean the same thing in any culture.

13

"You Should Hear the Screams" for Javier Baez

SO IF MARTIN PRADO, BUSTER POSEY, AND KRIS BRYANT play the game right, does that mean Javier Baez plays it wrong?

Baez flips his bat. Baez will wave his arms. Baez still shows the emotion of a kid, which is probably why so many kids love him. When they surveyed the players at the 2018 Little League World Series, Baez led the way in mentions as the kids' favorite major leaguer.

As Cubs radio announcer Ron Coomer said, "You should hear the screams when he comes to the plate at Wrigley."

You should also hear how much praise Baez gets from more traditional baseball guys—guys like his Cubs teammate Kris Bryant.

"He makes the hard stuff look easy," Bryant said. "That's why a lot of people like him... including me."

Bryant went on to explain that while there's no chance he would add the flair to his game that Baez constantly has in his, both ways of playing are perfectly acceptable. The flair is fine, if it's natural, which it obviously is with Javier Baez.

"I just be me," Baez said. "It's me out there."

Bryant's point was if he tried to play the game the way Baez does, it wouldn't be genuine and it wouldn't look right. But the same would be true if you forced Baez to play the game the way Bryant does.

What makes it work is that in the bigger picture, Baez does some very important things the way Bryant and Prado and so many others do. He plays hard and he plays with respect.

"I respect people who respect me," Baez said. "That's the way you get respect from everybody. A lot of people talk about how flashy I am out there, but I'm obviously not trying to show anybody up or any team up. It's just the way I play. It's my style, the way I learned to play the game."

There's room in baseball for that, especially for a player as talented as Baez. There's a need in baseball for it, in an era when those who run the sport are more and more understanding of the need to appeal to the next generation.

Baez can be that link, because while he plays with the flair and joy of a kid, he also plays with the instincts and the drive of the best who came before him.

"He could play baseball in any era," said Jason Heyward, a Cubs teammate whose own demeanor is more like Bryant's than it is like that of Baez. "He's a baseball player. He plays all over, plays it hard and tries to play it smart."

That's all anyone can ask. That's all anyone should ask.

Sure, Baez flips his bat after big hits. Sure, you'll see him with one hand in the air while the other is slapping a tag on a runner at second base.

Sure, he plays with flair.

"Flair is in the game now," former Cubs hitting coach Chili Davis said. "It's part of the game."

There's no doubt that part of the game has changed in the years since 1981, when Davis debuted as a 21-year-old outfielder with the San Francisco Giants. Part of the reason, as he said, is that the players in the game have changed.

Davis was born in Jamaica but from the age of 10 grew up in Los Angeles. And he was one of only two foreign-born players among the 35 who appeared in games for the '81 Giants. The other was Rennie Stennett, a Panamanian-born infielder who appeared in just 38 games.

Compare that to the 2018 Cubs, who featured players born in eight countries. Baez himself was born and raised in Puerto Rico, a Spanish-speaking U.S. territory with its own baseball culture, before moving to Florida when he was 12 years old.

He learned to play the game with enthusiasm and emotion, but he also learned to play it in a way that would be respected by everyone in the major leagues. Asked to name the players he followed most as a kid, Baez first lists Manny Ramirez, who he loved watching hit, and then Derek Jeter and Alex Rodriguez.

Like Ramirez, he attacks pitches and isn't afraid to show how happy he is when he connects. Like Jeter, he respects opponents and earns that respect back.

And like A-Rod, he showed great self-confidence at a young age. Baez joined his brother and some cousins in getting the Major League Baseball logo tattooed on the back of his neck when he was still in high school. Also in high school, he once responded to a high-and-tight pitch by pointing to the opposing dugout and saying, "You're going to pay."

A scout who was watching said Baez swung so hard at the next pitch that his back knee went to the ground. As for the ball, it ended up on a laser-like path headed for the scoreboard.

Baez still plays with that same enthusiasm, and while he's a lot less likely to point a finger at the opposition, he'll still have a right finger in the air as he slaps down a tag with the glove on his left hand. He'll still flip a bat if he hits the ball a long way, or call himself safe as he slides across the plate.

"He's not trying to show anyone up," Davis said. "He's not. If he was trying to show anyone up, he would be excessively upset when a guy gets him out. And he's not. He understands the game, and he plays the game.

"But when he's successful, he enjoys it."

When Davis played, hitters showed enjoyment at the risk of a fastball in the ribs the next time up. That's much less likely to happen now, although not unheard of, as Ronald Acuna Jr. can attest (more on that later). What's more likely is what happened with Baez and Amir Garrett, the Cincinnati Reds pitcher who gave up Baez's first career grand slam in May 2017.

Baez didn't flip his bat, but he did take an extra second or two before making his way around the bases.

A year later, almost to the day, Baez and Garrett met again, and this time Garrett struck him out. And this time, it was Garrett who showed he enjoyed his success, clenching his fist and shouting at Baez on his way off the field, letting out what

Cubs manager Joe Maddon later described as "a *Lion King*'s kind of roar." The benches emptied, but not much more came of it.

"I love Javy Baez as a player," Garrett told reporters that day. "I love the way he plays the game as a player, but if you're going to dish it, sometimes you have to take it. That's how it goes. There are no hard feelings. It is over with."

Was it really over? Maybe so. Baez and Garrett met again three months later, with Baez connecting for another home run. His celebration was nothing out of the ordinary, and Garrett had no visible reaction.

Baez said he knows the limits, what will and won't get him in trouble with opponents. It's fair to think he would have adapted to any era he played in, as Heyward said. It's also obvious he fits this era, and that baseball can use his more flamboyant style to appeal to those who might find parts of the game boring.

At Wrigley Field, every Baez at-bat is met with youthful screams from the crowd. The kids love the way he plays. That's clear.

What's interesting with Baez is that there doesn't need to be a young/old divide, no battle between old school and new school. Players who don't show nearly as much flair themselves can still appreciate Baez's instincts for the game, and the fact he draws a line at showing up opponents.

He got to the major leagues when he was just 21, and like most young players he still had things to learn. Even in 2018, in Baez's fifth major-league season, Maddon once pulled him from a game for failing to run hard to first base on a ground ball.

Baez admitted his mistake. And when he returned a day later with three hits including a home run, Maddon was smiling.

"He fessed up," Maddon said. "He knew he screwed up. He admitted to it. He goes out there and shows why he's one of the best players in the league."

Other times, Baez's teammates have told him when a bat flip seemed out of line.

"I think we know our limits," he said. "When we do something we're not supposed to do, a teammate will tell you. You've got to admit it if you were wrong. We're not trying to show anybody up. If it happens, we talk about it and move on."

Baez knows the kids are now watching him. He knows there will be many in the next generation who will want to play the way he plays.

"Everything keeps changing in the way that we play the game," Baez said. "We keep learning different things up here, and hopefully kids keep learning. I started focusing when I was 12 and I just kept getting good at it.

"It's me out there."

And that's a good thing.

14

Jose Urena, Keith Hernandez, and an Old-School View Fading Away

AS THE WIDESPREAD SUPPORT FOR JAVIER BAEZ SHOWS, THE unwritten rules don't always need to lead to a young-old divide. Baez may well be the symbol of the younger generation of players and fans, but plenty of baseball people who count themselves as old school also are unabashed Baez fans.

And when Keith Hernandez spoke out in support of what Miami Marlins pitcher Jose Urena did in August 2018, plenty of old-school baseball people were on the other side of the argument.

Here's what happened: Ronald Acuna Jr. was one of baseball's biggest emerging stars in 2018, a 20-year-old five-tool player who helped transform a 90-loss team into one that won 90 games and topped its division. When he came to the plate to start the first inning in an August 15 game at Atlanta's SunTrust Park, Acuna had become just the second player in the modern era to begin three straight games with a home run.

Urena was on the mound that night for the Marlins, and there was no chance he was going to allow Acuna to make it four straight. His first pitch of the game was a 97 mph fastball aimed directly at Acuna's left side. It hit Acuna on the left elbow, forcing him out of the game—while Urena was ejected.

Urena had no reason to be upset with Acuna, other than the fact that the kid was good and that all three of those leadoff homers had come in the same series off his Marlins teammates. Acuna was 8-for-13 with four home runs and nine RBI in the three games.

In another era, it probably would have been accepted—or even mandated by a manager—that a pitcher would come inside on him, make him move his feet, make him uncomfortable. In this era, Urena was mostly condemned around the game, except by Hernandez.

Hernandez wasn't even at the game. He was in Baltimore that night, calling the New York Mets game against the Orioles for the Mets' SNY network. In the sixth inning, with the Mets leading 8–1, the discussion in the Mets broadcast booth went to the game in Atlanta and the pitch from Urena.

"You've lost three games, he's hit three [leadoff] home runs, you've got to hit him," Hernandez told Wayne Randazzo, who was doing play-by-play that night. "I'm sorry. People are not going to like that. You've got to hit him, knock him down... I mean, seriously knock him down if you don't hit him."

Hernandez was right on one thing. People didn't like what he said.

"So by this way of thinking, Jacob deGrom should get drilled cuz he's the hottest pitcher on the planet? NO!" tweeted Braves

Hall of Famer Chipper Jones. "I'm old school just like this broadcaster, but these comments are waaay off base!"

Former major-league player and manager Bobby Valentine, speaking a day later on MLB Network, said, "If [Urena] was doing it intentionally, I think he should be banned from the sport. I think it's the worst thing about our sport. Some day it's going to kill someone. And I think it stinks."

Hernandez didn't back down from his comments, saying the next day he would have felt different if Urena had thrown the ball near Acuna's head.

"Sometimes you have to brush people back," he said on SNY. "I stand firmly by what I said, and I don't think the pitch was that terrible."

Hernandez said that if Acuna hadn't lowered his elbow, the ball would have hit him on the side and it's likely much less would have been said about it. He may be right about that. While many people were upset by the idea that Urena would throw at Acuna at all, it was the possibility of a great young player suffering a needless injury that got the most attention.

"What happens if they hit him there and it breaks his elbow and he's done for the year?" Braves manager Brian Snitker asked. "With what we're trying to accomplish here and where we're at [in a pennant race], there's no reason for that. I mean, this is a game."

It is a game, and I've even heard pitchers who have admitted throwing at hitters express regret that they could have endangered someone's career or even their life. But it's also true that part of the pitcher's job is to make the batter uncomfortable at the plate, and part of that usually involves making sure he doesn't believe he can just take over the inner part of the plate.

When Noah Syndergaard of the New York Mets went high and tight on Alcides Escobar of the Kansas City Royals with the first pitch of Game 3 in the 2015 World Series, Escobar and the Royals were upset. But just as many people accepted that the Royals had looked far too comfortable at the plate during wins in Games 1 and 2, and many of them gave Syndergaard credit for changing that right from the start in Game 3.

"I mean, I certainly wasn't trying to hit the guy, that's for sure," Syndergaard said in his postgame press conference. "I just didn't want him getting too comfortable. If they have a problem with me throwing inside, then they can meet me 60 feet, 6 inches away. I've got no problem with that."

There were two differences between what Syndergaard did in the World Series and what Urena did that night in Atlanta.

First, Urena's pitch to Acuna simply felt like sour grapes from a pitcher tired of watching a great player beat up on his team. Syndergaard's, as he said, was more about strategy, about putting a thought in the opponent's head that they couldn't dig in at the plate.

The other point is that Urena actually did hit Acuna and risked seriously injuring him (fortunately, nothing was broken and Acuna was back in the Braves lineup the next day). Syndergaard threw his 97.8 mph fastball to the backstop. It was up and in, but Escobar didn't have any problem getting out of the way.

Major League Baseball agreed there was a big difference. Syndergaard remained in the game, pitching the Mets to their only win in that World Series. Urena was not only ejected, but was also suspended for six games.

Syndergaard was within the rules, written and unwritten, as they are applied in the modern game. Urena's actions broke the rules, as administered by MLB, and also today's version of the unwritten rules, as proven by the statements by Jones, Valentine, and many others.

There was a time it was different. Most pitchers of yesteryear didn't actually hit many more batters than the pitchers of today—Bob Gibson and Nolan Ryan averaged fewer than 10 hit batters a season—but most hitters who played in earlier eras tell stories of being thrown at after having success.

"When I came up, guys would throw at you if you hit a couple home runs or got a couple hits off them," said Chili Davis, who debuted with the San Francisco Giants in 1981 and went on to an 18-year career. "They wanted to try to intimidate."

Davis stayed in the game after retiring as a player, becoming one of the most respected hitting coaches. He doesn't like everything about how the game has changed, but he never did like the idea of being thrown at simply because he was hitting well.

"If you can't get me out, walk me," Davis said. "When you start throwing at people and doing stuff like that, then you're taking people's careers into your own hands. That's not acceptable, especially with the money out there."

It wasn't acceptable when Cole Hamels threw at Bryce Harper when Harper was a rookie in 2012. Hamels admitted intent, saying he was trying to follow "old baseball" and give Harper something that said, "Welcome to the big leagues."

It was the wrong thing to say, and it helped earn Hamels a five-game suspension. But throwing at Harper simply because he was a top young star was also the wrong thing to do, even if Harper would later tell the *Washington Post* that he half expected it.

"I thought I would get it from somebody, just because of who I was," said Harper, who always took pride in understanding and appreciating old-school baseball. "But I didn't think it would be Hamels."

It was Hamels, and he didn't have many defenders. If anything, it was Harper who gained some respect that night, because after taking first base quietly when he was hit—not even looking at Hamels on the way there—he went to third on a single and stole home while Hamels was making a pickoff throw to first base.

That's how you get your revenge.

There are still old-school/new-school divides. But on this issue, the old-school position has fewer and fewer adherents.

15

Is There Still Room for a Purpose Pitch?

WHEN SYNDERGAARD WAS IN TRIPLE-A WITH THE METS, HIS pitching coach was Frank Viola, who pitched in the major leagues for 15 years beginning in 1982. Viola saw in Syndergaard a pitcher who didn't make hitters as uncomfortable as they should be when facing a guy that big (6'6", 240) who threw that hard (fastballs at 100–102 mph, sliders sometimes as hard as 95 mph).

Viola and other pitching coaches told Syndergaard he could be intimidating if he wanted to be. But he had to show it with his attitude, and he might need to show it once in a while by coming inside on a batter.

It's an issue pitching coaches and scouts talk about all the time, and there's definitely a feeling that today's pitchers don't use intimidation enough. They'll admit it's harder than it used to be, because some hitters react so dramatically to any pitch inside and MLB orders fines and suspensions if you hit a guy and they determine it's intentional.

Beyond that, more and more hitters come to the plate with padding on their front arm. Body armor, the pitchers call it. They're able to hang that elbow right over the inside part of the plate with no real fear that getting hit on the elbow will hurt.

Early in the 2018 season, I did a story for Bleacher Report on the increasing prevalence of hitters using the C-Flap, the helmet extension that covers a batter's jaw and lower face. When I posted the story to Facebook, a former major-league hitter responded with a comment that linked the C-Flap to the elbow guards.

"With the C-flap, hitters are taking away any fear they might have at the plate," wrote Randy Johnson, who was an infielder with the Atlanta Braves in the early 1980s and has worked as a major-league scout for many years. "That is one of the biggest differences in today's game. Pitchers can't intimidate any more. Hitters can crowd the plate with no risk or fear of being brushed back or retaliated against for swinging from their heels every pitch or standing on top of the plate. I would have loved to use one [C-flap], but I don't think it was allowed in the past unless you had a prior [hit by pitch] in the head or facial fracture. The hitters now own the inside part of the plate, and I doubt that will ever change with the lean toward helping the hitters any way possible. Bigger, stronger players, smaller strike zone and ballparks, juiced baseballs, dry/ultra light bats, lightning-fast infields, and very few pitchers that can locate a [fastball] all contribute to helping the hitters now. More [home runs] but fewer runs scored. Contact does make a difference and [I'm] not sure where the advantage is with today's hitting approaches. Why is the new wave style of 'all or nothing' so popular?"

Still, making hitters uncomfortable at the plate is a big part of a pitcher's job. So few pitchers are able to do it by throwing inside with a purpose that when I asked a former major-league pitcher if anyone now uses intimidation as a strategy, the answer was, "not intentionally."

In other words, the only guys who intimidate do it because they throw hard and they don't have great command. That's not really a strategy, and it wouldn't have fit with anything Bob Gibson or Pedro Martinez did.

Some writers have argued that pitchers from Gibson's era get more credit for intimidation than they should. Even Gibson questioned his reputation as a pitcher who used intimidation as a weapon, in a story Joe Posnanski did for MLB.com in early 2018.

"Ah," Gibson told Posnanski, "hitters don't get intimidated. That was just one of those things people said."

Perhaps, but when Gibson wrote his autobiography, *Stranger to the Game,* in 1994, he had a slightly different story.

"It was said that I basically threw five pitches—fastball, slider, curve, changeup, and the knockdown," Gibson wrote. "I don't believe that did me justice, though. I actually used about nine pitches—two different fastballs, two sliders, a curve, a changeup, knockdown, brushback, and hit batsman."

Don Drysdale understood the same thing.

"I never hit anybody in the head in my life," Drysdale told Murray Chass of the *New York Times* in 1987, "but you have to move them off the plate; you have to get them out of there.

This was part of the game and everybody accepted it as part of the game.

"The pitcher is trying to keep the hitter off-balance and keep his timing different from your timing. Once the hitter gets in sync, you're in trouble. I'm not condoning hitting anybody, but you want to back him off the plate. Pitchers [nowadays] don't know how to come inside."

Drysdale certainly knew how.

"Drysdale used to knock Willie Mays on his butt every other pitch," former big-league player and manager Buck Rodgers told Scott Miller of the *Los Angeles Times* in a 1993 story. "Then Mays would get up and hit a line drive."

So maybe it wasn't that easy to intimidate hitters. But coaches are always going to try to convince guys like Syndergaard to do it.

He learned from Viola, and he kept learning when he got to the major leagues. In 2015, Syndergaard was fascinated by the movie *Fastball*, which studied hard throwers from Walter Johnson to Bob Feller to Gibson and Nolan Ryan.

"I think of Bob Gibson a lot," Syndergaard said. "Listening to him in the documentary, he was the nicest guy in the world. But then he was a savage on the mound. Nolan Ryan seemed like a great guy, and he was an intimidating presence on the mound."

So in that 2015 World Series, when he watched the first two games and saw the Royals swinging at nearly every first pitch and having success with it, Syndergaard decided a purpose pitch to begin Game 3 might help.

He even telegraphed it, telling reporters at a press conference the day before the game: "It's something else being able to watch

Escobar walk up there and swing at the first pitch almost every single game. I have a few tricks up my sleeve that I'll be able to break out tomorrow night. I'm looking forward to it."

Then came the pitch, a 97.8 mph fastball that backed Escobar off the plate and flew all the way to the backstop.

Later that night, after he had won the game and addressed the reporters again, Syndergaard went to his phone and sent Viola a pointed text message.

"Hit *that* first pitch," the message read.

Viola loved it.

16

Kenley Jansen's Blacklist

AS A KID GROWING UP IN CURACAO, KENLEY JANSEN AND his friends had no unwritten rules. Or maybe they had one.

"You just play," Jansen said. "Have fun. We have fun. We play."

He signed with the Los Angeles Dodgers in 2004, a couple of months after his 17th birthday, one of many to leave the island that also gave baseball Andruw Jones, Didi Gregorius, Andrelton Simmons, and Ozzie Albies, among others. Jansen was a catcher then. Even after he moved to the mound five years later and even after he developed into one of the best closers in the major leagues, he would always maintain he could have made it as a catcher.

It worked out, and in January 2017 the Dodgers gave him a five-year, $80 million contract that made him one of the game's highest-paid relievers.

On the way there, he learned the unwritten rules.

"At certain innings, when you have a lot of runs, you can't steal a base," he said. "That's one thing we had to adjust to. Here, in the States, it's an unwritten rule that if you steal [with a big lead], you're going to get hit by a pitch. Or if you hit a homer and you don't run hard—not pimping it but just Cadillacing it a little, the pitcher won't like that, either.

"Those are two things that were different for us."

Jansen didn't hit many home runs in the minor leagues (15 in 953 plate appearances), which is one reason he became a pitcher. But one thing he decided when he moved to the mound was that he wasn't going to care how a hitter celebrated success against him.

"I really don't," he said. "I didn't make my pitch. Sometimes my execution was very poor, and you got me, or sometimes I've just got to tip my cap, if I made a really good pitch and you take me deep. But to be honest with you, that doesn't bother me. When a guy takes me deep, do whatever you want to.

"You're going to be on my blacklist regardless."

Wait a minute. It doesn't bother him, but if you hit a home run off him, you're on his blacklist?

Let Jansen explain.

"Because the next few times we play that team, the only guy I want to face is the guy that took me deep," he said. "That's my attitude."

Don't get this wrong. He doesn't want to face the guy again so he can throw at him.

"No, it's to get you out," he said. "Punch you out."

Punch out as in a strikeout, not in terms of throwing fists.

"I just want to punch him out," Jansen said. "I want to embarrass him. That's how I feel about it. So I really don't care, man.

Hitters do whatever they want to. Once you hit me, I'm going to have you on my blacklist to get you out, for the next few times."

There's a good chance he will. Jansen has faced more than 2,000 batters in his major-league career. He has struck out nearly 40 percent of them.

There's an even better chance Jansen won't throw at you. In nine big-league seasons combined, with all those batters faced, he hit just 17 batters. He's no head-hunter, that's for sure.

Even if one of his teammates has been hit by the other pitcher, Jansen doesn't believe in retaliation, at least not by throwing at someone in the other team's lineup.

"That's so stupid," he said. "That's another thing I really don't like. Sometimes the ball's going to come out of your hand and you're going to hit somebody. Like [in 2017], I hit the best hitter from the Chicago Cubs, Anthony Rizzo. I have a lot of respect for that man. I love seeing the way he plays. But I have to go in on him. He's a guy if you don't go in and you leave it over the plate, you're going to get beat."

Jansen knows that all too well. Through the end of the 2018 regular season, Rizzo had come to the plate 16 times against him. Rizzo had five hits, including a game-tying home run that cost Jansen a save, and a walkoff single. Jansen had retired him 10 times, including twice as the final out in a save. The other time, as Jansen said, he hit Rizzo with a pitch, obviously without intent, in the ninth inning of a tie game in the 2017 National League Championship Series.

"Same thing with Bryce Harper," Jansen said. "I don't think I've hit Bryce Harper, but I have to go in on Bryce Harper and

I hate that. If I hit them, I hate that rule that if I hit their best hitter they have to hit our best hitter. Stop being sensitive. That's how the game is."

Jansen actually did hit Harper once, also in a playoff game, also in the ninth inning when the game situation made it clear there was no intent.

For Jansen, this goes both ways. He doesn't want other pitchers throwing at Dodger hitters just because he hit one of theirs, but he also understands that most times when a Dodger gets hit, the pitcher wasn't intentionally throwing at him.

"Like [Justin Turner]," he said. "I'm not mad at teams that bust him in. You have to throw him in. He's the best hitter on our team. That's how you're going to get him out. He stands right on top of the plate. I really don't get that unwritten rule. I'm not speaking for any other pitcher, but for me, I'm not ever going to try to hit a batter on purpose. I'm going to try to get you out.

"In the ninth inning, when I pitch, I really don't care about anything but getting the hitters out. If I hit a guy, it's not going to do me any good. There's a guy on first, and I'm in trouble."

Jansen has strong opinions, but he isn't a rebel. He's not fighting against the way baseball is played in the major leagues, and he believes in most of what people say when they talk about "playing the game the right way."

"Those guys, I have high respect for them, and I love seeing how they play the game," he said. "One of my favorite guys I love to watch is Bryce Harper. He always plays the game hard. He always plays the right way. And he understands that sometimes we are coming in on him. If we hit him, he understands that we have to come in."

Through the end of the 2018 season, Harper had faced Jansen 14 times. Harper had four hits, including one home run in July 2015 at Nationals Park.

Did that put him on the blacklist? You'd better believe it. The Dodgers and Nationals met again a month later in a three-game series at Dodger Stadium. Twice in that series, Jansen faced Harper.

He didn't throw at him. But both times, he struck him out.

17

Torey (Just Like Earl)
Takes a Stand

ONE TEAM THAT CHANGED MANAGERS RECENTLY NOTICED
something interesting. When they came to a point in the job
interview where they explored a potential manager's philosophy, the older candidates all believed in the baseball tradition
that when your guys are getting drilled by pitches, your pitcher
retaliates and throws at one of their guys.

The younger candidates, almost to a man, didn't share that
belief.

It turns out it's not simply a young/old divide. When I asked
major-league managers in 2018 how they felt, 46-year-old Dave
Roberts of the Los Angeles Dodgers said he believes in pitchers
protecting hitters. And 40-year-old Kevin Cash of the Tampa Bay
Rays said he was willing to leave it up to his players.

Torey Lovullo wasn't willing to do that.

"I'm not a really big fan of taking a baseball and throwing it
at somebody as hard as you can," the 52-year-old Lovullo told
reporters early in the 2018 season, saying he had directed his

Arizona Diamondbacks pitchers not to retaliate in that way. "I know that there are some old-school baseball thoughts and some old-school baseball traditions that are still followed. I believe there's other ways that you can go out and operate and make things hurt when something like that happens."

The Diamondbacks followed their manager's directive. In a June 2018 game in Colorado, Rockies pitcher Brooks Pounders hit Diamondbacks star Paul Goldschmidt after Goldschmidt had homered four times in two games. Pounders' response was a 93 mph fastball that got Goldschmidt squarely in the ribs, and the response from many other teams would have been a missile directed at one of the Rockies' biggest hitters.

The Diamondbacks didn't respond, at least not in that way. And while their players weren't happy to see Goldschmidt hit, they seemed to support their manager, too.

"I think the game has matured and you understand that hitting guys isn't necessarily the best thing," pitcher Archie Bradley told MLB.com. "You can injure some guys and put guys in bad spots. But at the end of the day, you want to protect your guys and it was unfortunate and kind of uncalled for."

There are old-school thoughts and traditions that are still followed. But Lovullo's views weren't that different from those expressed decades before by Hall of Fame manager Earl Weaver.

Weaver always counseled his pitchers against retaliation, believing beanball wars and the resulting fights could lead to injuries his teams didn't need. He knew he had a good team, but he also knew the team was only good if his best players stayed on the field. If an Orioles pitcher threw at someone and the opponent responded by throwing at Brooks Robinson, the Orioles would not be better off.

Weaver wasn't alone, even in his own era.

In Game 3 of the 1981 ALCS, Oakland A's right-hander Matt Keough threw his very first pitch up and in on Yankees leadoff man Jerry Mumphrey. The Yankees responded by winning the game and finishing up a sweep that sent them to the World Series. But they didn't respond with a similar knockdown pitch to any of Keough's teammates.

Bob Lemon was the Yankee manager at the time, and like Weaver he didn't believe in retaliation. Lemon had been a Hall of Fame pitcher himself, and he never forgot the feeling that he might have seriously hurt a batter he was throwing at.

"That's why I'll never order a pitcher to knock down a hitter," Lemon said.

Keough knew the feeling, especially after he saw the look in Mumphrey's eyes.

"I so regretted it," he said years later. "His life and family could have been destroyed."

Keough's regret only grew when he was traded from the A's to the Yankees in June 1983. He arrived in the middle of the season and needed black cleats (the A's wore white). The player who wore the same size shoe and generously offered Keough his cleats was... Jerry Mumphrey.

But Keough was doing what pitchers in his era normally did when he threw at Mumphrey in 1981. Keough had watched the Yankees take advantage of A's pitching in the first two games of the ALCS in New York, and he wanted to make a point from the start that the A's wouldn't be pushed around.

It was notable that the Yankees didn't retaliate with a similar pitch, just as it was notable when Weaver's Orioles stayed away from beanball wars.

In 1976, after Reggie Jackson joined the Orioles as a free agent, Jackson expressed his disgust when teammate Lee May was hit twice in the same game against the Royals, taking the second one in the head.

"If we don't hit someone tomorrow, by God, I'm walking off this team," Jackson said after the game. "I know Earl's philosophy about this sort of thing, but this time it's different. We've lost eight in a row and you can't win if the other team takes a 100-RBI guy away."

Jackson even said he was willing to "fight them all"—the entire Royals team!

As it turned out, Orioles reliever Grant Jackson did hit Royals shortstop Freddie Patek (in the back) the next day. The Royals even thought it might have been a reaction to what Jackson said.

The Royals' reaction was just as interesting. Starting pitcher Dennis Leonard told reporters he considered retaliating, but that Patek told him not to bother. Instead, the Royals' retaliation came in the form of an 8–4 win.

"Reggie inspired the hell out of 'em, didn't he?" Royals manager Whitey Herzog said.

Leonard's explanation after the game was interesting.

"When they did hit Freddie, I thought about brushing somebody back but it would look so obvious," he said. "Then Freddie said, 'No, don't do that.' And really, it would be insane to stir something like that up.

"If [Grant Jackson] was trying to intimidate our hitters, it didn't work. He intimidated them eight runs' worth."

Torey Lovullo, who was 10 years old, growing up in California, and presumably not aware of anything going on between the Orioles and Royals, probably had no opinion at the time.

But two decades later, he was advocating the same approach.

Lovullo might be an outlier in being so vocal about his feelings, but he's not alone in believing that throwing at hitters intentionally is a strategy best left in baseball's past.

"I'd never tell a pitcher to hit somebody," said Dave Martinez, who took over as Washington Nationals manager in 2018. "Never."

Martinez prefers to retaliate by finding a way to make the pitcher pay for putting a runner on base.

"I was hit plenty of times in my career," he said. "I'd get to first base and try to steal second base, steal third base, and score a run."

Martinez, who turned 54 in September 2018, was one of the younger managers in the game. But as Roberts and Cash proved, it's not always a young-old divide.

Consider what 64-year-old Joe Maddon said a couple of weeks later.

"I'm not in favor of any pitcher throwing at a hitter," Maddon said. "And I've never ordered any pitcher to hit anybody."

Many managers have said that, but what Lovullo said went a step further. Even a manager who isn't ordering a beaning may well look the other way when his pitchers decide to hand out a version of baseball justice. For years, pitchers have handled this themselves, sometimes at the direction of position players on their team.

Is that changing? Will the Lovullo edict become more widespread in the game?

As with so many of the other unwritten rules, we'll just have to watch and see.

18

When It's Still an Eye for an Eye

RICK SUTCLIFFE PITCHED 18 YEARS IN THE MAJOR LEAGUES and faced more than 11,000 hitters. He hit only 46 of them.

And some of those were on purpose.

In fact, Sutcliffe said, he had a simple rule when a player on his team got hit and it seemed intentional. His own unwritten rule, if you will.

"I never had a manager tell me to hit anyone," said Sutcliffe, who retired in 1994 and has since worked as a baseball announcer on television. "But if one of my guys got drilled, I'd go to him and say, 'Who do you want me to get?' I need those guys driving in runs for me."

It was about protecting your teammates, and in many ways it still is. The Tampa Bay Rays weren't happy with having several of their players hit in a late September 2018 series against the New York Yankees, and in the sixth inning of an already one-sided game at Tropicana Field, Rays reliever Andrew Kittredge went up and in to Yankees catcher Austin Romine.

It was, as Marc Topkin wrote in the next morning's *Tampa Bay Times*, a "badly executed attempted retaliation" by a 28-year-old rookie. What followed from Yankees lefty CC Sabathia was a well-executed retaliation pitch that hit Rays catcher Jesus Sucre in the left leg.

"That's for you, bitch," Sabathia yelled toward the Rays dugout.

What made it all more interesting to many of those watching was that it was Sabathia's final start of the season, and if he had stayed in the game for two more innings he would have qualified for a $500,000 incentive bonus for pitching 155 innings.

"I don't really make decisions based on money, I guess," Sabathia said when reporters alluded to the bonus. "Just felt like it was the right thing to do."

By traditional baseball standards and the unwritten rules that have governed the game for years, there was no question it was the right thing. Sabathia's teammates understood and seemed to appreciate it, and Sucre seemed to understand as well.

"You can go ask [Kittredge]," he said when reporters asked. "He's the one who decided to do it."

Notice that he blamed his own pitcher, because the unwritten rules also say Kittredge was in the wrong for throwing his apparent retaliation pitch near Romine's head. By those same rules, Sabathia was in the right to show Kittredge and the Rays the high and tight pitch wasn't acceptable.

"I have a lot of respect for CC and if he feels he should need to hit somebody and he did it, I have more respect because he protects his players," Rays outfielder Carlos Gomez told reporters.

"That's how the game is supposed to be played. You protect your guys, they're going to protect you."

The only problem with doing so is that Major League Baseball doesn't always see things the same way. Sabathia was ejected from the game and was suspended for five games. Kittredge was suspended for three games, as MLB followed precedent in levying a heavier suspension on the pitcher who threw at a batter after umpires issued a warning to both teams.

"MLB has changed the calculus," Washington Nationals right-hander Max Scherzer said. "If you're on a good team and you're in a pennant race, you're always cognizant you could be suspended and miss a start. That's the thing you always have to ask yourself today."

In Sabathia's case, there wasn't much to consider, at least not as far as his team was concerned. The Yankees were already far ahead in the game, and since it was the final week of the season, his suspension wouldn't be served until the 2019 season began.

But what if it had been earlier in the season? What if it had been Scherzer, clearly his team's best starting pitcher, in the position of wanting to retaliate but concerned about a suspension?

As much as his hitters might appreciate him standing up for them, would they be happy missing out on a playoff spot by one game and knowing their Cy Young pitcher missed a start trying to protect them? Then again, will they be happy if they feel pitchers from the other team are able to get away with anything?

"Retaliation is a strong word," Los Angeles Dodgers manager Dave Roberts said. "It's taking care of your guys. We play 162 games, and you have 25 guys, or more than that over the course of a season. You have to know each one has each other's back. Pitchers and hitters, that's something you have to have."

It's more complicated now than it was in Sutcliffe's day, or when Doug Brocail was a rookie with the 1993 San Diego Padres. The details are a little fuzzy two decades later, but Brocail tells the story of pitching the day after one of the Padres' big hitters had been targeted by an opponent.

"I had heard from the moment I got into baseball, take care of the guys who score runs for you," Brocail said.

He was a nervous 25-year-old kid, but he walked up to his team's slugger and asked who on the other team he should hit.

"Don't worry about it," the slugger told him.

Very nice of him to say that, Brocail thought.

"I did it, anyway," he said.

It happens, even now, and in most cases everyone on both teams understands and accepts exactly why it happened. As long as the pitcher keeps the targeted pitch low—away from the head, preferably somewhere around the hips—the batter drops his bat and goes to first, with nothing else said.

The unwritten rules have been followed. The game has policed itself.

And just as in Sabathia's case, the pitcher who retaliated is seen as sticking up for his hitters, which helps his standing in the clubhouse.

"There's a right way to do it," Houston Astros pitcher Justin Verlander said. "It's about where you hit a guy. You see it all the time with veterans, where they get hit, they know it, and it's done the right way, and they just take it and go to first base and they don't say a thing about it. And then it's done. Message sent, message received, everyone's aware, and that's the end of it. That's the way this game's always been policed.

"If you start going high, near his head, then you've got some issues."

And if you're throwing at someone, you'd better hit him. Jack Morris, who pitched in the big leagues for 18 years, proudly claims he never missed.

"Seven for seven," Morris said. "They wore a baseball. They never once screamed, either. They knew why they were hit."

Morris said protecting his players went far beyond retaliating when an opposing pitcher threw at them. He got more upset at opposing baserunners who went in too hard at second base, risking injury to second baseman Lou Whitaker or shortstop Alan Trammell.

"I couldn't afford to get those guys hurt," Morris said.

Baseball has also changed the calculus on slides at second base, changing the rules in 2016 after Chase Utley broke New York Mets shortstop Ruben Tejada's leg with a takeout slide in a playoff game the year before. But even that didn't settle every issue. It may have even made things worse in some ways, because infielders believe the new rule will protect them and don't work on getting out of the way of baserunners.

So when Adam Eaton of the Nationals went in hard to break up a double play on the first day of August 2018, Mets second baseman Phillip Evans took the throw from shortstop Amed Rosario and made no attempt to avoid Eaton. Eaton's slide conformed to the new rules, as the Mets announcers noted on

SNY and as MLB confirmed. But the slide also left Evans with a broken leg, and Mets manager Mickey Callaway insisted the next day that it was "a little too aggressive."

Three weeks later, the Mets let Eaton know exactly what they thought, throwing one pitch up and in and another that hit him on the backside.

"If they want to hit me or throw at me, that's fine," Eaton said. "I'll take it. Just keep it below the shoulders and above the knees, I'll be fine with it. Put me on first base, I'm good."

Eaton took first base without a word, and the Nationals considered the issue resolved.

The situation was different early in the 2017 season, when the Boston Red Sox took offense at Manny Machado, then with the Baltimore Orioles, sliding hard into Red Sox second baseman Dustin Pedroia. The problem was that instead of hitting Machado in the butt, as Mets pitcher Zack Wheeler did with Eaton, Red Sox pitcher Matt Barnes nearly hit Machado in the head.

As Verlander said, that's a big no-no. Even Barnes' Red Sox teammates didn't defend his actions. Pedroia told reporters he texted Machado.

"I just told him I had nothing to do with that," Pedroia said. "I just told him that's not how you do that. I said sorry to his team. If you're going to protect guys, you do it the right way."

And as much as baseball might try to take over by changing rules and issuing suspensions, many players will still believe protection is necessary. Many will also believe that protection can come only from a pitcher throwing at a hitter.

As Curt Schilling told reporters in 1997, he learned it soon after he signed his first professional contract.

"The manager said he would kick my butt if I didn't protect my teammates," Schilling said.

Schilling was speaking out because he was upset his Phillies teammates didn't immediately retaliate after a Hideo Nomo fastball knocked Scott Rolen out of the Phils lineup. It was the third time Nomo had hit Rolen in 11 plate appearances that season (and two of the other plate appearances resulted in a double and a home run).

Rookie Wayne Gomes was in the game at the time, and Schilling believed it was Gomes' job to hit one of the Dodger stars in response.

"In the most primal sense, those guys [the Dodgers] represent the enemy, trying to take food off our table," Schilling said. "They've taken away our meal ticket. And Scotty's a meal ticket for all of us."

Whether it was Schilling or someone else in the Phillies clubhouse, the message got through. A day after Rolen was hit by Nomo, Phillies starter Matt Beech hit Dodgers catcher Mike Piazza in the leg. Piazza, who suggested to reporters he expected to get hit, took first base after a stare at Beech.

"I don't like to get hit, but what can you do?" Piazza said to reporters. "Just remember and see what happens."

With the Dodgers in a pennant race, Piazza didn't want to risk a suspension by charging the mound. His teammates agreed with him.

"They've got nothing to lose," Eric Karros said, referring to a Phillies team that was 35 games under .500. "We've got everything to lose."

As much as baseball might want to, there's no way to eliminate every perceived need for pitchers to protect hitters.

Pitchers are always going to hit batters. Hitters are always going to take offense if it happens too often.

Everyone understands what can happen next.

When Clint Hurdle came to Pittsburgh to take over as Pirates manager in 2011, one of his goals was to have his pitchers take back the inside part of the plate. The 2010 Pirates had lost 105 games with a 5.00 team ERA that was the worst in the major leagues. Hurdle knew that the more they threw inside, the more success they would have. But he also knew that a corollary effect of this strategy was that they were sure to hit more opposing batters.

So in addition to talking to his pitchers, Hurdle spoke to his hitters. Be prepared, he told them, because if our pitchers hit more guys, there's a good chance more of you get hit in retaliation.

By 2013, the year Hurdle's Pirates turned things around and became a playoff team, Pirates pitchers led the National League with 70 hit batters. It was no surprise to Hurdle that Pirates hitters were hit 88 times, also the most in the league.

Hitters understand, and in many cases they don't mind. They know their pitchers need to work inside.

When Chicago Cubs starter John Lackey hit four Chicago White Sox batters in a July 2017 game at Wrigley Field, everyone including Lackey and the rest of the Cubs could figure out a Cubs batter was probably going to wear one. Sure enough, White Sox reliever Chris Beck hit Ian Happ with a pitch.

"Their retribution was obvious," Cubs manager Joe Maddon said. "I had no argument."

Kevin Kiermaier remembers seeing two of his Rays teammates hit Derek Jeter with pitches in 2014. And he remembers being the first batter up for the Rays after the second one.

"I knew I was gonna try to get hit," Kiermaier told reporters later. "They missed me, a guy ended up getting ejected. I expected it, I'm okay with that. I get how a game works.... I would have had no problem if he would've hit me. He ended up missing. The game went on. But there's other times when guys are out of line and you have to defend yourself."

Hitters only get upset if they think their own pitcher was out of line, throwing at a hitter simply out of spite after giving up home runs. If it's their pitcher protecting them, as Brocail was doing in his rookie year, that pitcher gets immediate respect. Sometimes he even gets more than that.

"I think the guy ended up picking up my clubhouse dues for the rest of the year," Brocail said.

19

Is There a Statute
of Limitations on Revenge?

THE TEXAS RANGERS WAITED SEVEN MONTHS TO GET BACK
at Jose Bautista. They waited through six regular season games
and most of a seventh in 2016 to retaliate for Bautista's flamboyant bat flip in the 2015 American League Division Series.
They waited until the eighth inning of their final scheduled
game against Bautista's Toronto Blue Jays, when they had hard-
throwing Matt Bush on the mound.

That's when Bautista got a pitch in the ribs.

"Gutless," Blue Jays manager John Gibbons said after the game.

Gutless or fully justified? There's a way of thinking in baseball
that suggests the crime of disrespect comes with no statute of
limitations. You get your revenge whenever you can—and whenever you want to.

Early in the 2018 season, a fascinating video showed up on
the Internet showing manager Terry Collins and his New York
Mets players arguing with umpire Tom Hallion during a May
2016 game against the Los Angeles Dodgers at Citi Field. It was

the game where Mets pitcher Noah Syndergaard was ejected in the third inning for throwing a 99 mph fastball behind Dodgers second baseman Chase Utley, in obvious retaliation for the Utley slide that broke Mets shortstop Ruben Tejada's leg in the 2015 playoff series between the two teams.

"Tommy, that's bullshit and you know it," Collins says on the tape, referring to Syndergaard being thrown out of the game. "You've got to give us a shot! You've got to give us a shot!"

"Terry, listen to me and hear what I'm saying," Hallion responds. "You get your shot. You had your shot right there."

"Why don't we get a shot, Tommy?" Collins screams.

"Because that makes it worse," Hallion says. "Terry, that makes it fucking worse."

"I know it," Collins says. "But MLB did nothing to that guy! Nothing!"

"You know I can't control that," says Hallion. "I'm telling you, our ass is in the jackpot now."

In other words, the umpires felt they had no choice but to eject Syndergaard, because they and everyone else watching understood the Mets pitcher was absolutely throwing at Utley. The Mets were upset their player got hurt on Utley's slide, and they were doubly upset that Utley never served a suspension for the play. MLB initially suspended Utley for two games, but it was withdrawn without ever being served.

Even without a suspension, Utley didn't play in the two games that followed the Tejada injury. He pinch hit in the ninth inning of Game 5, but with a one-run lead the Mets weren't going to risk putting him on base. Instead, they threw at him seven months later.

As it turned out, Utley got some revenge of his own. After Syndergaard was gone from the game, the Dodgers second baseman hit two home runs to lead his team to a 9–1 win.

Hunter Strickland waited more than two years to get back at Bryce Harper for a perceived slight.

Harper hit two long home runs off Strickland in the 2014 National League Division Series between Harper's Washington Nationals and Strickland's San Francisco Giants. They were big home runs, and Harper stopped to watch them before circling the bases.

Not much was said about what Harper did, but Strickland obviously noticed. He didn't face Harper again until May 2017. With two out and nobody on in the eighth inning that day, he threw a 97.8 mph first-pitch fastball aimed directly at Harper's right hip.

Harper seemed to know immediately what it was about. He pointed his bat at Strickland, then tossed the bat away and charged the mound.

"History," Nationals television analyst F.P. Santangelo said immediately.

"He hit me in the right spot, so I do respect him for that," Harper said. "He didn't come up and in toward my face like some guys do, so I respect him on that level."

But Harper thought Strickland was wrong to do it, because it had been so long and because the Giants had gone on to win the 2014 series despite Harper's home runs.

"It just wasn't relevant," Harper said. "Like I said, it was three years ago, over a thousand days ago I guess. I don't know why he's thinking about it."

Strickland never addressed why he was thinking about it. He followed the pitchers' code of not even admitting he was throwing at Harper, probably hoping MLB would go easier on him if he didn't acknowledge the obvious. As it was, he still got suspended for six games (while Harper got four for charging the mound).

Was it worth it? Only Strickland can answer that question.

Did he wait too long? Baseball history suggests it's never too late to right a perceived wrong.

Pitchers never forget. In September 1975, in the final game of his 17-year Hall of Fame career, Bob Gibson allowed a grand slam to Pete LaCock. It was nearly the final batter Gibson faced. He got the third out of the inning, on a Don Kessinger groundout, and that was it. Except the way LaCock told the story years later, he and Gibson were playing in an old-timers game in Kansas City sometime in the 1980s. Bob Feller was pitching, but when Gibson saw LaCock at the plate, he insisted on taking the mound—and he drilled LaCock in the back!

"I've been waiting *years* to do that," Gibson yelled.

And the unwritten rules don't include anything saying that's too long to wait.

20

When Even Teammates Don't Like It

WHEN A PITCHER THROWS AT A HITTER AND HE IS SEEN AS following the unwritten rules, the pitcher gains respect. And not just from his teammates.

In many cases like that, the batter understands and takes his base with nothing else said.

But when a pitcher throws at hitters for the wrong reasons, or when he throws in the wrong spot—i.e. too close to the batter's head—not even his own teammates will feel bound to defend him.

Take what happened in the final week of the 2009 season. The Minnesota Twins and Detroit Tigers were involved in an American League Central race that would go to a one-game play-off in Game 163, but the dispute that day wasn't between teams.

Apparently upset that the Tigers twice took second base on defensive indifference in a game the Twins led 8–2, rookie Twins reliever Jose Mijares threw a fastball behind Tiger shortstop Adam Everett's back. When Tigers pitcher Jeremy Bonderman responded by hitting Twins outfielder Delmon Young on the leg, Young knew exactly who to blame.

He got up and pointed, but not at Bonderman or anyone else with the Tigers. He pointed at his own dugout, at Mijares.

"He needs to understand how to play the game," Young told reporters later. "This isn't the minor leagues over here.... You can't throw behind their players and expect nothing to happen."

Young's teammates seemed to feel the same way, with shortstop Orlando Cabrera calling what Mijares did "a selfish act" and Twins manager Ron Gardenhire calling his Tigers counterpart, Jim Leyland, to apologize.

"Our pitcher lost his cool out there and made a mistake," Gardenhire told reporters. "[The Tigers] did what they had to do, and it's over with and they did the right thing, what they had to do, and we screwed up."

In Mijares' case, his screwup only cost Young a painful fastball to the leg. Young was angry, but he stayed in the game and was back in the lineup the next day, too.

That's better than what happened to Derek Bell when he was playing for the Houston Astros in 1995.

Doug Brocail was pitching for the Astros against the Atlanta Braves that day, and in the second inning, Brocail gave up a long home run to Braves outfielder David Justice.

"It was probably eight rows from hitting the back wall behind the seats," Brocail remembered years later. "If it's in Boston, it's probably one seat shy of hitting that red seat that Ted Williams hit. He hit the ball and went, 'Whewww!' I didn't like it, so later in that game I smoked him."

He sure did, for no reason other than being upset by the home run and Justice's reaction to it. The problem with that was that Bell ended up paying the price.

Justice was the Braves right fielder that day. Upset that Justice was hit, Braves starter Steve Avery responded by throwing at the Astros right fielder: Bell.

Avery followed the unwritten rules. He didn't throw at Bell's head. The pitch hit him in the left thigh. That's normally a safe spot to get hit, but in this case Bell eventually needed surgery to repair a blood clot in the thigh and didn't play the rest of the season.

"I ended up being the bad guy," Brocail said.

That said, he still doesn't regret hitting Justice.

"Absolutely not," he said. "If he had just hit the ball and run around the bases, everything would have been fine. I still to this day think I would probably plunk him."

To this day, hitters get upset if they get plunked simply because their own pitcher was upset about giving up a long home run. They get upset with their own pitcher, though, as opposed to the pitcher who threw at them in retaliation.

"I know sometimes I have to wear it," said Eric Thames, who knew he could become a target for retaliation in 2017, when he hit 31 home runs and was batting in the middle of the order for the Milwaukee Brewers.

It can get complicated, because if the whole team thinks an opposing hitter is showing them up, they're going to be fully behind any one of their pitchers who retaliates by throwing at him. But if that pitcher is responding to a perceived slight that his teammates don't feel, or if he is simply hitting a batter because he's tired of giving up runs, he can have big problems with his own hitters.

In the first case, it's the wildly celebrating hitter who is seen as breaking the unwritten rules. In the second, it's the wildly sensitive pitcher.

It can make all the difference in the world.

21

Don't Call Me Coach
(But You Can Come Talk to Me)

MOST OF THE UNWRITTEN RULES CHANGE WHEN PLAYERS change. They're the ones who decide something offends them, and they're the ones usually in charge of doling out baseball justice.

Managers can tell their pitchers they don't believe in retaliation, as Torey Lovullo does now and as Earl Weaver did years ago. But it's still the pitcher with the ball in his hand.

Managers can decide some offense screams out for retribution, but it's still the pitcher who must do it. Mickey Lolich wrote in his 2018 book *Joy in Tigertown* that he always refused such a request, because he felt so bad about seriously injuring a batter he threw at in a Babe Ruth League game while growing up. Lolich wrote that when Billy Martin managed him with the Detroit Tigers in 1971–73, Martin threatened to fine him.

"It will cost you $100 if you don't drill him," Martin told him. "And if you don't do it the second time I tell you to, it will cost you $200. It will keep going up."

"I didn't care," Lolich wrote. "I refused to throw at hitters."

For the most part, though, the manager is the boss. He's also not called a coach. That's one of the first things every player learns after getting into pro ball. You call the manager by his first name or his nickname, or you call him "skip" (short for skipper). You don't call him "coach."

But just because you're on first-name terms with him doesn't mean he's not in charge.

The best managers have the ability to stay out of the clubhouse and still stay on top of everything that goes on in there. Veteran infielder Martin Prado never forgot what Hall of Fame manager Bobby Cox said in an early meeting when Prado was a rookie.

"You won't see me around this clubhouse," Cox told his team. "This is for the players. But if you see me around, you'd better worry, because something's going on."

Before games, Cox would be in his office or in the dugout, or in a little room he used just behind the Braves dugout at Turner Field.

"He created this environment where everyone respected him," Prado said. "Everyone wanted to do something to earn his respect."

Watch the next time you see the Braves play during the day. You won't see any player or coach with his sunglasses over the top of his cap. It was a Bobby Cox rule, one Brian Snitker kept going when he became Braves manager. You don't cover up the Braves' "A" on the front of the cap.

It's all about respect.

The best managers end up forming close relationships with many of their players, but they stop short of ever being buddy-buddy with them. The best managers gain so much respect from their players that the players don't even want to cross them.

Juan Samuel tells the story of coming to Sparky Anderson's Tigers as a 33-year-old veteran in 1994. Samuel quickly became friends with Cecil Fielder, and the two of them liked to go out for a drink every now and then. The Tigers had a rule banning alcohol on team flights, but Sammy and Cecil would sneak a bottle of vodka and some orange juice onto the plane in brown bags.

They thought they were getting away with it until one day Sparky called the two into his office.

"I know what you're doing," he said. "And it's okay. But don't let any of the young players see it."

From that day forward, Samuel and Fielder didn't bring alcohol onto a Tigers plane again.

"We felt like we'd be letting Sparky down," Samuel said. "And we couldn't do that."

Anderson was from a different era, but the story tells you a lot about the player-manager relationship, right up until the present time. Managers will always allow veteran players a little leeway, but they and the players understand what lines can't be crossed.

Player-manager relationships have changed over time, but the need for a manager to understand his players in order to get the most out of them has never changed.

"I treat all of my players the same, and I treat all of my players differently," Jim Leyland liked to say during his 22 seasons as a major-league manager.

All of his players mattered to him. But some of them responded best to a kick in the butt, while others performed best with a pat on the butt.

"My job is to push them when they need to be pushed, to hug them when they need to be hugged, to believe in them always, and set a culture where they'll believe in themselves and they'll prioritize winning," A.J. Hinch said in a press conference a few minutes after his Houston Astros had won Game 7 of the 2017 World Series.

When Joe Maddon took over the Cubs before the 2015 season, one of the first things he did was fly to Puerto Rico to meet Javier Baez. Baez had just just turned 22. He had played just 52 games in the major leagues.

"The big thing was to get to know him because he was going to be part of the future soon, to develop a relationship with him," Maddon told Tom Verducci, describing the visit for Verducci's book *The Cubs Way: The Zen of Building the Best Team in Baseball and Breaking the Curse.*

Maddon has always had unique ways to reach his players. In 2018, he started something new, arranging to go to dinner with a player when the Cubs had an off day or a day game.

"I really like the concept a lot," Maddon said. "Any time you can get with your players away from the field, in a more casual setting, in a more social setting, I think the conversation has a chance to reach a level it can't reach in my office, or it can't reach walking around the outfield. I take some of my coaches with me. I like to take the more entertaining coaches."

Maddon turned 64 years old in 2018, but his style of managing fits the modern game and modern players. He's also old enough to remember when the game was different.

"I remember I had one manager who said, 'There's 25 of you and only one of me, so you'd better learn me,'" Maddon said. "I think if there's 25 of you and one of me, I need to learn 25 of you. But that was directly said to us, and I'll never forget that. You learn from the people you had in the past that you never want to be like, and that was one right there."

Maddon has long believed in listening to his players, back to the days when he coached and managed in the Angels system. Clint Hurdle, who turned 61 in 2018 and is from the same generation, has adapted over time.

"Society has changed," Hurdle said. "I have a 33-year-old daughter and that's very helpful, because she's the same age as some of the players. I talk to her about how to communicate with them."

When Torey Lovullo took over as the Diamondbacks manager in 2017, he understood that modern players weren't as willing to just accept anything the manager told them. Lovullo had great respect for Anderson, who was his first manager with the Tigers in 1988, but a decade later when he was in his final year as a player with the 1999 Phillies, Terry Francona showed him a different way.

"He kind of took it to the next level, where he explored what I was thinking and what I was feeling, and I enjoyed that,"

Lovullo said. "I think the players today enjoy that, too. Players have become very expressive and they want to share, and that's important. Really what I've said from Day 1 here is what the player thinks matters. I really believe that. That's how this game has evolved."

Lovullo now likes to think of his Diamondbacks as an organization that listens to its players. He points to how the team treated Jake Lamb when Lamb was about to come off the disabled list in May 2018. Rather than simply decree whether Lamb would do a rehab assignment in the minor leagues before returning, the D-Backs asked him what would best get him ready.

Lamb chose the rehab, telling the team he wanted to get in the routine of preparing for a game, rather than staying at the training complex and getting more at-bats.

"There are certain guidelines, team rules," Lovullo said. "But in an interaction with a player who feels like he's not getting the right amount of playing time, in my generation you'd probably get thrown out of the manager's office immediately upon walking in there. Today, when someone comes into my office, I sit 'em down and let 'em purge. I try to relate to them. And then I tell them what my thoughts are."

And what would Sparky have done?

"He would have said, 'Young man, I've been in this game a long time. You see where your locker is? Go sit in front of your locker, and I'll get you when I need you.'"

22

The Kids Are Alright
(and It's Okay to Hear from Them)

ONE DAY IN LATE MAY OF 2018, JUSTIN UPTON SAT IN THE
Los Angeles Angels clubhouse and glanced up at a television. The
MLB Network was playing, as it does regularly before games in
every major-league clubhouse. Scrawling across the bottom of
the screen were names of the projected top picks in baseball's
amateur draft, which was a little more than a week away.

Thirteen years earlier, Upton himself had been the first overall pick in the draft, chosen by the Arizona Diamondbacks out
of a Virginia high school in June of 2005. There was no MLB
Network then. The draft wasn't shown on television. It was
conducted by conference call. The players chosen weren't well
known, although in the years to come they would be. After Upton,
players like Ryan Braun, Troy Tulowitzki, Ryan Zimmerman, Jay
Bruce, Jacoby Ellsbury, and Alex Gordon were taken in the first
round.

Upton signed for a $6.1 million bonus. He was in the major
leagues just two years later, at age 19.

And compared to those still-to-be-drafted players scrawling across the screen in front of him, he was still relatively anonymous.

"They're under more of a spotlight than I ever was," Upton said. "I almost feel sorry for them. They're not allowed to be kids. When I came to the big leagues, I could go have lunch without anyone noticing. I could roam around Arizona. I could do whatever I wanted."

At least until he got to the ballpark.

In 2007, rookies were still expected to be rookies, in the traditional sense.

"When I first came up, you didn't talk," said Peter Moylan, who debuted with the Braves in 2006 and was back pitching for them in 2018. "You just sat in your locker, sat on your hands."

"That was so hard for me, because I have such an open personality," said Sergio Romo, who came to the big leagues for the first time with the 2008 San Francisco Giants. "I didn't say a word. No knock against the veterans we had, but it was, 'Congratulations, you've made it to the big leagues, but you haven't done anything yet.'"

It was part of the unwritten rules of the game, as it had been for years and years. Justin Verlander came to the big leagues in 2005, and after he'd had a few years of service time he thought nothing of looking over at a mouthy rookie and saying, "Hey rook, know your place."

By 2018, those unwritten rules had changed. Verlander said he wouldn't issue such a directive anymore.

"A lot has changed," Verlander said. "It's younger guys acting like veteran guys. When I came up, if a young guy hit a homer and pimped it, he was going to get hit. If a veteran did it, it was okay. I think a lot of it may be because of MLB Network and the availability of social media. Guys get sensationalized at a younger age. You get here and you've already got all this hype. You're not a nobody."

For the most part, the younger players still rely on the their older colleagues to teach them the unwritten rules and the way to act in the big leagues. There are still stories of older players taking a just-arrived rookie to go shopping and then putting down his own credit card to make sure the kid has nice clothes to wear on the team plane. But there are also stories like the one that became public in July 2018 with the St. Louis Cardinals.

Bud Norris was a 33-year-old reliever for the Cardinals, and Jordan Hicks was a hard-throwing 21-year-old who jumped straight from Class A to the major leagues. Norris took it on himself to make sure Hicks understood he had to show up on time and do all the things required of a big-league player.

Norris didn't always express himself in the best way, sometimes yelling across the clubhouse at Hicks. Hicks didn't always appreciate what Norris was trying to do for him.

And Cardinals manager Mike Matheny, who had empowered Norris to become the leader of the bullpen, backed his veteran in an interview with Mark Saxon of The Athletic.

"I think the game has progressively gotten a little softer," Matheny said. "Man, it had some teeth not that long ago."

The Cardinals fired Matheny four days after the story appeared, not because of that quote but because his team was underachieving. But in a game where there are more and more young players and those players have more and more status, Matheny probably didn't help himself by encouraging veterans to show those "teeth."

Young players today feel much more free to express themselves, in the clubhouse and on the field. Freddie Freeman, who at 28 qualified as a veteran on a young Braves team in 2018, marveled at how one of his young teammates reacted to getting a hit in a regular-season game at Yankee Stadium.

Freeman was raised in a culture where emotions were to be kept in check. He learned from Chipper Jones, and he learned you were supposed to be the same guy when you went 0-for-20 as you were when you were rolling along with 10 hits in your last 20 at-bats.

Now he sees 20-year-old Ronald Acuna Jr. raising his arms and celebrating at first base after beating out an infield hit.

"I'm all for that," Freeman said. "It's fun. It's a breath of fresh air. He's just excited to be playing baseball. Believe me, I'm never going to do that, but I'm not going to be the one taking anything away from these guys."

Veterans like Freeman will still take a young player aside if they see a celebration getting out of hand, or if it crosses the line to where it could be seen as disrespecting an opponent.

But fun? If there was an unwritten rule before against showing you had fun playing the game, that's gone now. Even most of the veteran players are fine with that.

"The whole game trending younger is great for the excitement," Moylan said.

Most older players in the game today welcome the change. Some have even worked hard to encourage young players to feel comfortable, as CC Sabathia has done with the New York Yankees.

In a story Marc Carig wrote for The Athletic in 2018, Sabathia said he never wanted a young player to experience what he had when he joined the Cleveland Indians as a 20-year-old in 2001.

"You didn't feel welcome," Sabathia said. "It was hard. I didn't enjoy my first couple of years in the big leagues."

Sabathia told Carig he got hassled by older Indians players simply for sitting on a sofa in the middle of the clubhouse. He said he was determined to change the culture when he got older. As it turned out, Sabathia became a veteran as baseball's overall culture was changing, and he helped the Yankees lead the way.

"They made it a point to say, we don't care if you're a rookie," Yankees outfielder Aaron Judge told Carig. "We don't care if you're a free agent or if you've been traded over. You have the pinstripes on, you're going to help the team. We're going to do whatever we can to make you comfortable so you can go out there and perform at your best."

More and more, young players have become key to lineups and rotations. More and more, rookies don't feel alone in their own clubhouse.

"There's a lot more young teams," said Jason Heyward, who was 20 years old when he debuted in 2010 but by 2018 had begun to feel like an older veteran at 28. "Clubhouses are getting younger. It's hard for somebody that's 24 and has two years in or is 25 and has three years in to tell a guy just coming up that 'You need to calm that down.' That's just part of the game. Things evolve."

The Braves team Heyward joined included a 37-year-old Chipper Jones, a 33-year-old David Ross, and a 33-year-old Troy Glaus. The Braves starting pitcher in Heyward's first game was 36-year-old Derek Lowe.

"They wanted me to laugh," Heyward said. "But I'd sit at my locker. For the most part, that was the only place I sat. Speak when spoken to. Got on the plane last. I remember the day Troy Glaus pushed me and said, 'You're good now, you can go.' I came up with some veterans and some good veterans.

"And they had it way worse than I did when they were coming up."

Baseball's attitude toward younger players had already begun to change by the time Heyward arrived in the big leagues. The changes continued, and after the 2016 season MLB's new Collective Bargaining Agreement put an end to some of the rookie hazing practices that had become standard over the years.

While teams could still have rookie dress-up days, they were no longer allowed to force players to dress up as women or do anything else that would be considered offensive.

Baseball was simply adapting to societal norms, but the effect was to change some rituals that had gone on for years. Veterans had to find other ways to encourage team bonding, and to get young players to understand the way they were expected to act.

"I had Eddie Guardado around my first spring training," said Drew Storen, who was a first-round draft pick out of Stanford when he showed up in Washington Nationals camp in the spring of 2010. "He told me to respect the guys who have been around. I always had to have gum in my back pocket for him. Did he ever chew the gum? Probably not, but that wasn't the point."

It turned out the Nationals would release Guardado before spring training even ended that year. He wouldn't ever pitch professionally again, but Storen never forgot the lessons he learned that spring.

That passing on of knowledge and of the game's tradition still happens, but as rosters and clubhouses get younger, the rookies of today aren't always as willing to defer to their elders.

"I came up with Cal and Eddie," said Gregg Olson, who in 1988 joined an Orioles team where Cal Ripken Jr. and Eddie Murray were established stars. "They were never rude, but other guys would let me know, 'Hey kid, sit down and zip it. Nobody wants to hear you.' I didn't say a word for a year."

And Olson was the American League Rookie of the Year in 1989.

It wasn't just a matter of not talking. Young players were expected to defer to veterans in the clubhouse, on team planes and buses, and even in training rooms and batting cages.

Mike Greenwell fought Mo Vaughn at the batting cage when Vaughn was a Red Sox rookie in 1991, at a time when Red Sox veterans thought Vaughn was taking liberties before he'd earned them. The two later went on to become good friends, and were inducted into the Red Sox Hall of Fame on the same day.

When Tino Martinez took over as hitting coach of the Miami Marlins in 2013, he was a very respected player who was working as a coach for the first time. It didn't go well, in part because in his view the Marlins' young players weren't following etiquette in the batting cage before games.

The way Tino described things in a story by Ken Rosenthal, then of Fox Sports, three Marlins players didn't pick up balls in the cage, and didn't take it kindly when he told them they should. That's how Martinez had learned to do things. That's the way he'd seen things done with the Yankees, who were filled with veteran stars.

"If Bernie Williams is hitting in front of me and I'm waiting with Paul O'Neill or whoever, there are no questions asked," Martinez told Rosenthal. "You help pick the balls up, and the next guy hits. Whoever is hanging around helps pick the balls up. It's standard."

When Martinez saw Marlins players standing around letting others pick up the balls, he called them out on it. He admitted to using some rough language when he did it, but nothing you wouldn't hear in a baseball clubhouse every day. He also admitted grabbing Derek Dietrich by the jersey when Dietrich refused to help. And when it came to a head and the players complained about Martinez being too combative, Martinez resigned.

Sometimes, though, the young player is taught a lesson that sticks. Take what happened to Noah Syndergaard in his first major-league spring training with the New York Mets.

The Mets were playing an intra-squad game. Syndergaard wasn't scheduled to pitch in the game, but as a rookie he was expected to be in the dugout supporting his teammates. Instead, he was in the clubhouse sitting down to eat.

Mets captain David Wright got his at-bats, and when he was done he grabbed his bats to take them back to the clubhouse. There was Syndergaard sitting there at a table with his lunch in front of him. Wright told Syndergaard to get back to the dugout, immediately. Veteran pitcher Bobby Parnell, who also walked into the clubhouse, picked up Syndergaard's lunch and dumped it in the trash.

Syndergaard learned his lesson. It's fine for a kid to eat, but as a young player he was expected to be in the dugout supporting his teammates first. Not everyone is in the dugout at all times during every game, but if a young player is missing there had better be a good reason.

"I'm hungry" is not a good reason, especially not from a kid who hasn't yet paid his dues.

23

Watch What You Say (or Tweet)

WHENEVER VETERAN PLAYERS OF TODAY COMPLAIN ABOUT how young players act when they come to the big leagues, someone invariably brings up the other side of it.

"I'm sure glad social media didn't exist when I was young," the older player will say.

And then he'll look up from his iPhone or iPad.

Some players pride themselves on ignoring Twitter and Facebook and Instagram, just as some players in the past never wanted to read the newspapers (or said they didn't). Others keep a Twitter feed for marketing purposes but don't touch it themselves, preferring to hand it off to an agent or other aide.

But in the modern world, no one escapes social media entirely. Every player knows it is there, for better or for worse. It's nice for players to be able to communicate directly with fans. It's not so nice when somebody's camera phone captures an embarrassing moment and that person shares it instantly around the world.

It's even worse when your own Twitter feed includes some-thing truly offensive, as happened to three young players in 2018.

Milwaukee Brewers reliever Josh Hader was enjoying his first trip to the All-Star Game when a Twitter user dug into his past and found tweets that were racist and homophobic. The tweets were six and seven years old, posted when Hader was still in high school, but that hardly excuses them.

To his credit, Hader never claimed his account had been hacked. He never even asked how in the world someone found the old tweets. He apologized, as fully as anyone can at a time when he is also admitting to once typing the vilest of words into his phone.

"I was young, immature, and stupid," Hader said.

Soon enough, he wasn't alone.

The same day Sean Newcomb was taking a no-hit bid into the ninth inning for the Atlanta Braves, someone else was digging into his Twitter past and finding racist and homophobic tweets from his high school years. Newcomb also apologized, as did Trea Turner of the Washington Nationals when his own ugly old tweets were shared on the Internet.

"I'm truly sorry for what I said, and I want to take full responsibility for that," Turner said at a Nationals Park press conference.

The unwritten rules of the game are simple here. Be careful of anything you say or do, because somebody will find out and then everybody will know. And if anything like that does come out, offer up as quick and sincere an apology as you can.

Be careful with what you say. Be careful with what you post. Be careful, even, with what you "like."

In the aftermath of Game 2 of the Yankees-Indians division series in 2017, when Yankees manager Joe Girardi didn't use a replay challenge when he should have and the Yankees lost the game, a Yankees fan went on Instagram and posted: "Let's hope Joe's contract is not renewed after the season. He's a complete imbecile." No big deal, except someone noticed that the account @_thecubanmissle54 "liked" the post. @_thecubanmissile54 is Aroldis Chapman, the Yankees closer.

It's possible some public relations person runs Chapman's account for him. It's possible Chapman hit the wrong button. Girardi accepted Chapman's apology and his explanation it was "an accident."

In 2015, Pablo Sandoval got in bigger trouble over an Instagram "like." A Red Sox blogger checking out the social media site noticed Sandoval had "liked" two provocative pictures of a young lady. No big deal, except he did it during a game! Sandoval admitted it, saying he had gone to the bathroom and checked his phone on the way. The Red Sox benched him for a game as punishment.

But even in the era before social media got so big, players had to watch how they acted off the field. Even then, stories would circulate if a player got in a fight in a bar, or even if a group of players were hanging out in the clubhouse while a game was going on.

Players aren't required to be in the dugout at all times, and there are often good reasons for a player to go to the clubhouse.

Some pitchers who are charting games find it easier to do off the television feed. Some players will watch video, either of their at-bats or of pitchers they may face. A designated hitter may ride an exercise bike to stay loose between at-bats.

All good reasons, and all perfectly acceptable. But sometimes what happens in the clubhouse finds its way into print or onto the Internet, and sometimes it can be embarrassing.

After the Red Sox collapsed in September 2011, going from having the best record in the league at the end of August to not even making the playoffs, a story appeared in the *Boston Globe*. Among other things, it said pitchers Josh Beckett, Jon Lester, and John Lackey spent much of the month eating biscuits and fried chicken and drinking beer in the clubhouse during games. In many fans' minds, it became the reason the Red Sox collapsed, even though some things like that have gone on in many clubhouses. The biggest difference with the 2011 Red Sox was that someone actually talked about it.

"I can guarantee that these guys drank less beer than a lot of other teams," manager Terry Francona wrote in the book he did with Dan Shaughnessy, *Francona: The Red Sox Years*. "I was most disturbed by the idea that stuff wasn't staying in the clubhouse. They weren't protecting each other. If somebody was drinking, they weren't drinking a lot. I'm not saying it's right, but I was more disturbed by our lack of unity."

Francona understood that if stuff like that was getting out, it meant the team had bigger problems than just a few pieces of chicken or a few bottles of beer.

The 1999 Mets had a similar issue, when it came out that Rickey Henderson and Bobby Bonilla were in the clubhouse playing cards during a game in the National League Championship Series against the Braves. The Mets lost the series in six games.

Bonilla explained in a radio interview years later that Henderson was upset with manager Bobby Valentine for double-switching him out of the game in the eighth inning.

"Rickey says to me 'Bo, get the deck of cards, let me just relax my mind.' And we had actually played cards all year long," Bonilla said on WFAN. "He was so upset, so we can't say 'So what,' because you don't want anything escalating after, so I just took care of the problem and let it go."

But for years, many Mets fans came to believe that Henderson and Bonilla cared so little about an important game that they were playing cards as it went on.

24

Why Can't We Be Friends?

GREGG OLSON WAS JUST 21 YEARS OLD WHEN HE DEBUTED with the Baltimore Orioles in 1988, less than three months after the Orioles made him the fourth overall pick in that summer's amateur draft. Olson joined a team that began the season with a 21-game losing streak and finished it with a 54–107 record, but he quickly enjoyed personal success.

By the following June, Olson was the closer on a team that surprised everyone with 87 wins. He was the American League's Rookie of the Year, and he was named on ballots for both the Cy Young and Most Valuable Player awards.

His career was off to a fine start, and he would collect 95 saves before he turned 25.

Oh, and he could get Chili Davis out. Davis was in his thirties by then, an established major-league hitter. But in eight plate appearances against Olson between 1989 and '91, he had never gotten a hit.

One day during batting practice, Olson saw Davis approaching him and wanting to talk. Nice guy that he is, Olson said hello.

Then he felt Dwight Evans behind him. Evans was 39 years old then, and in his final big-league season, the only one he would spend with any team other than the Boston Red Sox. He was an Oriole and he was about to teach Olson a lesson in the unwritten rules.

"Dwight Evans grabs me by the shirt and drags me away," Olson remembered years later. "He says, 'What are you doing?'

"I'm like, 'I'm 24 years old, and that's Chili Davis,'" Olson said.

"He just wants to see if you're a nice guy," Evans said. "If he knows you're a nice guy, you're not going to hit him. He's trying to make friends with you so he'll know you're not going to hit him and he can be more comfortable in the box."

"Hey," Olson replied. "I'll still hit him."

Perhaps, but Olson faced Davis two more times before Chili retired. The result: a two-run single and a double.

Who knows if it had anything to do with feeling more comfortable, but Olson learned that in the generation before his, fraternization between opponents was strongly frowned upon.

There's actually a rule against it. It's not even an unwritten rule. It's right there in the rulebook, Rule 4.06:

"Players in uniform shall not address or mingle with spectators, nor sit in the stands before, during, or after a game. No manager, coach, or player shall address any spectator before or during a game. Players of opposing teams shall not fraternize at any time while in uniform."

The written rule hasn't been changed, but the unwritten rules on fraternization sure have been. Get to any big-league game early and you'll see players from the two teams mingling as one team is finishing batting practice and the other is getting ready to start. Players greet ex-teammates or guys they grew up with or guys who have the same agent or just someone they've come to know along the way.

There are hugs. There are smiles. There are laughs.

Players go talk to coaches or managers from the other team. Before most games, the two managers will chat amicably.

And old-timers sitting in the stands shake their heads. The old-timers get even angrier when they see opponents chatting during games.

It wasn't always that way.

"For me, once the game starts, I'm going to battle with you, and I don't need to be talking to you," said Juan Samuel, who played 16 years in the major leagues and has worked as a manager and coach with the Phillies, Tigers, and Orioles. "I remember Cecil Fielder told me when I first came to the Tigers, 'You used to come to first base and not say hi to anybody.' I said, 'What was I going to talk to you about?'"

Samuel and Fielder became best friends. So, when they met on the field after Samuel had moved on to the Blue Jays, there was some conversation.

"I used to tell him, 'I'll talk to you later, because I'm not sticking around, I'm going to steal second base,'" Samuel said. "But [the fraternization] is one of the things I hate."

Samuel talked about times when he was coaching third base and his team would have a runner on first base. He'd be ready to give the signs, but he'd look across the diamond and see his baserunner in deep conversation with the opposing first baseman.

"To us, the first thing we did when we got to first base was pick up the coach and get the sign," Samuel said. "Then you'd check the outfielders to see where they were playing. Now they're at first base talking to the first baseman and then they're at second base talking to somebody and you're just trying to get their attention."

25

When There's a Fight,
You'd Better Be There

PLAYERS TODAY MAY BE MORE LIKELY TO BE FRIENDS, BUT
friends can still fight.

Maybe one team thought there was a call for retaliation and
the other team thought it went too far. Or somebody's emotions
simply got out of control, something was said and in the heat of
an emotional game, someone took it the wrong way.

Tensions rise and something sets off the fuse. Before you
know it, both teams are on the field, going at it.

Now what?

The unwritten rules dealing with fights are actually pretty
simple. For the most part, everybody agrees what should happen
and what shouldn't. They may argue about the value of fights or
the need for them, but once they break out it's pretty standard
what the rules are.

First, if your teammate is involved, you'd better be out there
on the field. You don't have to be throwing punches, but you'd

better be there. Trying to help break it up or simply trying to make sure your side isn't outnumbered is perfectly acceptable.

Throwing sucker punches isn't.

Baseball fights may look like melees, but most of the guys you see all over the field are pushing, pulling, or just standing around trying not to get hit. As for the ones who want to throw punches, the key is that those need to be delivered face-to-face and one-on-one.

And any player out there has to remember that in today's game there are multiple camera angles of everything, and after a fight every one of those angles will be checked. They'll be checked by the umpires and the MLB office, which is responsible for handing out fines and/or suspensions.

They'll also be checked by players on both teams, who will be looking to see who should be the subject of frontier justice. Sucker punchers aren't acceptable, and they also aren't soon forgotten.

Think about what happened in August 2017 in Detroit, when the Tigers and Yankees got into it. The fight began at home plate between Detroit's Miguel Cabrera and New York's Austin Romine, but while they were rolling around on the ground, the Yankees' Gary Sanchez ran up and sucker-punched Cabrera.

Sanchez later said his "instincts" just took over, but nobody accepted that as an excuse.

"He can do whatever he wants," Cabrera said. "But if he wants to punch me, let it be face-to-face."

Later in the same brawl, Sanchez also sucker-punched the Tigers' Nicholas Castellanos. MLB gave Sanchez a four-game suspension, later reduced to three.

The problem with being seen as a sucker-puncher is that the reputation doesn't go away easily. Word gets around the league quickly these days, whether through video replays on television or text messages between friends.

Proper etiquette also says you fight with your fists. Fifty years later, people still talk about the time Giants Hall of Fame pitcher Juan Marichal hit Dodgers catcher John Roseboro over the head with his bat. In that key game between rivals in the 1965 pennant race, Marichal had knocked down the Dodgers' Maury Wills, and Dodgers pitcher Sandy Koufax responded by throwing one over Willie Mays' head. Marichal responded to that by throwing at Ron Fairly. In today's game, there would have been warnings issued well before this point, but in 1965, things were different. It took all of that for umpire Shag Crawford to warn both teams. Anyway, rather than have Koufax retaliate and risk ejection, the Dodgers' response came from Roseboro, when Marichal was batting. On a throw, back to the mound, Roseboro buzzed him, throwing it right past Marichal's head.

That started the brawl, which was fine except Marichal stunned everyone by clubbing Roseboro with his bat. Then and now, that's not cool.

"I was afraid he was going to hit me with his mask, so I hit him with my bat," Marichal said the next day.

Roseboro needed 14 stitches. Marichal was ejected, suspended for eight game days, and fined a then-record $1,750 (about $14,000 in today's money). Roseboro also sued Marichal and settled for $7,500.

Fortunately, no player since has used his bat as a weapon. Helmets are another story. When Bryce Harper went after Hunter Strickland at AT&T Park in May 2017, Harper took off his helmet and threw it in Strickland's direction.

26

If You Show Someone Up, There's Going to Be Trouble

ONE OF THE BIGGEST STORIES OF THE 2017 SEASON IN Boston began with a single word.

Hall of Fame pitcher Dennis Eckersley was working the NESN television broadcast on June 29, the same night Red Sox pitcher Eduardo Rodriguez made a rehab start for the Double-A Portland Sea Dogs. Rodriguez didn't have a great night, giving up six runs (five earned) on nine hits in three innings.

The Red Sox were playing the Twins that night at Fenway, and after Rodriguez finished his work, NESN put his pitching line on the screen.

"Yuck," Eckersley said.

It was just one word, but David Price didn't like it.

It was a getaway day. The Red Sox were flying to Toronto that night after the game, to begin a series with the Blue Jays. Team broadcasters regularly travel on team planes, and Eckersley was part of the NESN crew on the Red Sox charter that night.

As later reported in the *Boston Globe*, Price was standing toward the middle of the plane when Eckersley boarded. Since the broadcasters sit in the back of the plane on Red Sox flights, Eckersley had to pass by where Price was standing. When he got there, Price stepped in front of him and began shouting.

"Here he is—the greatest pitcher who ever lived!" Price said, according to Dan Shaughnessy's report in the *Globe*. "This game is easy for him!"

When Eckersley tried to respond, Price continued.

"Get the [expletive] out of here!" he said.

Price's actions were popular with some of his teammates, some of whom applauded.

"I stand up for my teammates," Price told reporters after his next start. "Whatever crap I catch for that, I'm fine with it."

There are many ways to show someone up. It can be as simple as taking someone on in front of others, as Price did. It can be flipping your bat in someone's face, or standing at home plate admiring a home run. It can be stealing bases when you're ahead by eight runs.

Some third-base coaches will tell you that if they have a big lead in the late innings, they won't send a runner home unless he's going to score standing up. If he's going to have to slide, they'll hold him up, play station to station.

Don Mattingly played the game the right way. But when Mattingly was managing the Marlins against the Dodgers in May 2017, he took offense when Dodgers shortstop Corey Seager swung at a 3-0 pitch with his team ahead 5–0 in the seventh inning.

When the teams later traded hit batters and the benches cleared, Mattingly said he didn't approve.

"[Marlins closer A.J. Ramos] gives up a homer and a guy gets hit. It looks bad," Mattingly said. "But also they're up 5–0 and swinging 3-0. If they want to actually count stuff. They can say however they want it. But when they swing 3-0, up 5–0 going into the eighth, you can put it however you want."

Not everyone will agree on what lead qualifies as big. Back in 1993, when Mattingly was still playing, his Yankees team held a 6–0 lead in the sixth inning one night at Tiger Stadium. When Pat Kelly stole second base, Tigers manager Sparky Anderson took offense. Television cameras showed Sparky yelling across the field at Buck Showalter, who was managing the Yankees at the time. Later, after the Tigers had come back to win the game 7–6, Showalter said he had just wanted to get a seventh run.

Sparky never publicly criticized Showalter by name, but he didn't buy that reasoning. In an interview later that season with the *New York Times*, Sparky equated running with a big lead to swinging 3-0 in the same situation. He didn't approve of either one.

"I was raised one way," Sparky said. "You have never seen me run five or more runs ahead. Not once. And you ain't going to do it to me. If you do, I'm going to pay you back. I promise you that. There is a thing in this game: honor. It will always stay with me and I'll never give it up.

"Four runs, you can hit a grand slam and tie me. But you'll never see me hitting [with a 3-0 count] five runs or more ahead. You don't cherry-pick on the other team. You don't take cripples—3-0, he's struggling; he's got to lay the ball in there. Don't do it to the man. He's got a family, too."

In other words, don't show anybody up. If you do, be ready to face the consequences.

27

The A-Rod Rules
(or Stay off My Mound)

ALEX RODRIGUEZ HIT 696 HOME RUNS IN HIS CAREER, BUT
it was hardly a smooth ride. He was twice outed as a user of
performance enhancing drugs, and in 2014 he became the first
player to serve a full-year suspension for using PEDs.

But even when he wasn't breaking baseball's drug rules,
A-Rod had a way of finding himself in trouble over unwritten rule violations. One of the strangest came in 2010, when
Rodriguez ended up in the middle of controversy because he
ran over the mound as he was going across the infield.

Who does that? Only Alex.

And he claimed to have no idea what he did wrong.

It was a mid-April day game in Oakland. The Yankees were
playing the A's, and with one out in the sixth inning of a game
the A's led 4–2, Rodriguez reached on a base hit. Robinson Cano
was the next hitter, and he hit a foul ball down the left-field line.
A-Rod had passed second base and made it almost all the way
to third by the time the ball was ruled foul. On his way back to

first, A-Rod not only went over the mound, he stepped on the rubber as he passed it.

Dallas Braden, the A's pitcher, was not impressed.

"Get off my mound," he yelled.

Cano grounded into a 3-6-1 double play, and after Braden recorded the final out of the inning at first base, he turned to yell again at A-Rod as he went back to the dugout. When the game was over, Braden unloaded again, this time to reporters.

"If my grandmother ran across the mound, she would have heard the same thing he heard—period," Braden said. "That's the way I handle the game and the way I handle myself on my workday. That's just the way it is. I would never disrespect anybody like that."

There was more.

"I don't care if I'm Cy Young or the 25th man on a roster," Braden said. "If I've got the ball in my hand and I'm out there on that mound, that's not your mound. You want to run across the mound? Go run laps in the bullpen. That's my mound."

And...

"I don't go over there and run laps at third base. I don't go over there. I don't spit over there. I stay away. You guys ever see anybody run across the mound like that? He ran across the pitcher's mound, foot on my rubber. No. Not flyin'."

And one more.

"The long and short of it is it's pretty much baseball etiquette. He should probably take a note from his captain over there, because you don't run across the pitcher's mound in between an inning or during the game. I was just dumbfounded that he would let that slip his mind."

The best part of the story: part of A-Rod's response was that Braden talked a lot for a guy with 17 career wins. Fair enough, but a couple of weeks later, Braden got his 18th career win by throwing a perfect game against the Rays.

His grandmother, Peggy Lindsey, was in the stands for the perfect game. And she got quoted, too.

"Stick it, A-Rod," she said.

He didn't need to stick it. He just needed to stay off the mound.

It's pretty simple. There are places you go and places you don't. The base coaches don't really need to stand in the designated spots near first and third base, but if they inch so close that they might be looking to steal signs, someone is sure to complain.

The on-deck batter doesn't need to stand right on the mat they put in the on-deck circle, but he's not supposed to stray too far from it, either. Get too close to the plate, and the pitcher is going to take offense. Same goes for the first batter of the inning, while the pitcher is throwing his warm-up pitches.

Some hitters like to get a better view of the pitcher's delivery or how his pitches move, but if they get too close the next pitch might move right into their ribs. Players quickly learn where to stand and even where to walk—watch how a right-handed hitter approaching from the first-base dugout will circle around behind the plate rather than crossing in front of it to get to his batter's box.

Players are particular about their equipment, too. You'll often see a guy using someone else's bat or mitt, but only with permission. Some hitters are so particular about their bats that they don't want anyone else touching them.

Ichiro Suzuki has always carried his bats in his own special case, all the way back to when he played in Japan. The case, which can hold eight bats at a time, is shockproof and moisture-free.

"He dresses like a rock star and he carries his bats around in a case like a rock musician with a guitar," Yankees pitcher Boone Logan told David Waldstein of the *New York Times* in a 2012 story.

28

The Jeter Rules
(or Acting Can Win You
More than an Oscar)

IT WAS THE MIDDLE OF SEPTEMBER IN 2010, AND THE
Yankees and Rays were in a tight race for first place in the
American League East. The Yankees were half a game ahead,
so every game was huge. And in the seventh inning on September 15, Derek Jeter came to the plate against Rays reliever Chad
Qualls with one out, the bases empty, and the Yankees trailing
2–1. The Yankees needed to get the tying run on base, and Jeter
knew it. So when Qualls' first pitch was inside and ticked off the
knob of Jeter's bat, he made like it hit him and started heading
for first base. Longtime Yankees athletic trainer Gene Monahan
even came out of the dugout to give Jeter "medical attention" on
his left hand. The Rays knew Jeter didn't really get hit, but Jeter
was able to convince home-plate umpire Lance Barksdale he did.

"Give Derek Jeter an Oscar. And extra MVP consideration,"
Phil Rogers wrote in the *Chicago Tribune*.

Gary Shelton, writing in the *Tampa Bay Times*, wasn't as
impressed.

"Suddenly, Jeter was in absolute agony," Shelton wrote. "It was like he was one of those Western outlaws who had just had the gun shot from his hand by Wyatt Earp. There hasn't been this much torment to a guy's hand since Darth Vader sliced off Luke Skywalker's in the Empire Strikes Back."

Shelton went on to say his problem was with the theatrics, not that Jeter was willing to take first base when he wasn't actually hit. He understood, just as Jeter understood and Rays manager Joe Maddon understood, that a player's responsibility in such a case isn't to the truth. It's not a crime, not even a baseball crime, to take what's given to you even when you technically don't deserve it.

"It hit the bat," Jeter admitted after the game. "[Barksdale] told me to go to first. I'm not going to tell him, 'I'm not going to go to first,' you know? My job is to get on base."

He got on base, and Curtis Granderson followed with a two-run home run that gave the Yankees the lead. As it turned out, Dan Johnson hit a two-run home run off Phil Hughes in the bottom of the inning and the Rays still won the game.

Maybe that's why Maddon could later joke about it.

"There's several thespians throughout baseball," Maddon said. "I thought Derek did a great job, and I applaud it, because I wish our guys would do the same thing."

It usually doesn't work anymore, now that Major League Baseball allows the use of instant replay to challenge calls. If Jeter's acting job happened today, there's no doubt Maddon would have challenged and little doubt the call would have been overturned.

But as we saw in the 2017 playoffs, even in today's game players could get away with it. Lonnie Chisenhall didn't get hit by a Chad Green pitch in Game 2 of the ALDS in Cleveland, but home-plate umpire Dan Iassogna said he did. Yankees catcher Gary Sanchez seemed to know the ball actually hit the knob of Chisenhall's bat, but Yankees manager Joe Girardi inexplicably declined to ask for a challenge.

On that play, Chisenhall didn't do any acting (which probably should have been a tipoff to Iassogna and Girardi that he wasn't really hit). He just stood there. He didn't admit the ball had hit his bat and not his hand, but why should he?

As he said after the game, "I'm not the umpire."

He's a player. As Jeter said, his job is to get on base. You're not supposed to cheat to do it, but what he did wasn't cheating. It was gamesmanship.

Nothing in the written or unwritten rules says it's not okay.

And then there's what Jose Tabata of the Pirates did in June 2015. Max Scherzer of the Nationals was one out away from a perfect game when Tabata came to the plate in the ninth inning at Nationals Park. In fact, Scherzer was one strike away when the count went to 0-2. He missed with a slider and a fastball to go 2-2, and Tabata fouled off a slider and two more fastballs. Scherzer's next pitch was another slider, off the plate inside. And you can see clearly on the replay that Tabata lowers his front elbow, covered by padding, and makes sure the pitch hits him.

On the Nationals' MASN broadcast, F.P. Santangelo was incredulous.

"I got hit by more pitches than most, and there's no way I'm leaning into a pitch down 6–0 when a guy has a perfect game going," F.P. said. "I would never do that."

F.P. got hit by pitch 25 times in a season, so he ought to know the etiquette.

As for Scherzer, his immediate answer was that he was disappointed in himself rather than upset with what Tabata did.

"It was a slider that just backed up, and it hit him," Scherzer said. "I don't blame him for doing it. I mean, heck, I'd probably do the same thing. So it was a pitch that got away from me, and it hit him."

The written rules of baseball say a batter isn't entitled to first base when he "makes no attempt to avoid being touched by the ball." In reality, umpires almost never apply the rule, and some guys make it part of their game to get on base by turning into inside pitches and allowing themselves to get hit. Pitchers don't love that, especially when the guy gets hit on what pitchers like to describe as the "body armor" some guys put on their front arm when the go to the plate.

Home plate umpire Mike Muchlinski could have ruled Tabata wasn't legally hit, since he certainly made no attempt to avoid the pitch. Muchlinski didn't do that.

"He tried to throw a slider inside, and it didn't break. It stayed right there," Tabata said. "And he got me. He got me on the elbow, on the protection [his elbow pad]. I want to do my job."

Scherzer went on to do his job, getting Josh Harrison on a fly ball to left field to complete his first career no-hitter (he'd throw another one later that season against the Mets). A no-hitter is special, but a perfect game is legendary. In all the time Major League Baseball has been played, there have been just 23 of them (through 2018).

Other pitchers have lost perfect games in the ninth, and even with two out in the ninth. But Scherzer was just the second pitcher to lose a perfect game by hitting a batter with two out in the ninth. The other was George "Hooks" Wiltse of the Giants (his brother was "Snake" Wiltse), on July 4, 1908. Like Scherzer, Wiltse went to a 2-2 count before he hit Phillies pitcher George McQuillan on the shoulder. Like Scherzer, Wiltse ended up with a no-hitter, although he had to pitch 10 innings to finish his.

Sadly, there's no video showing whether McQuillan leaned into the pitch.

29

Every Player Can Be "Johnny Hustle"

WHEN MANNY MACHADO ARRIVED IN THE MAJOR LEAGUES as a 20-year-old rookie in 2013, it was easy to compare him to Alex Rodriguez. He was a big, athletic infielder from Miami. He was a shortstop who was moving to third base.

He even wore A-Rod's No. 13 on his back.

"Same number, same actions," the scouts said.

But when he got to the Baltimore Orioles that year, Machado didn't act like another A-Rod. He was "sincere," Orioles manager Buck Showalter said. He had a knack for doing and even saying the right thing.

"I'm Manny," Machado said. "I'm going to be myself. I came in, and I didn't step on anyone's toes. I came in to just be myself and play baseball."

What happened to that guy?

Five years later, Machado seemed more like A-Rod than ever. Maybe worse, because A-Rod was never heard saying, "I'm not the type of player that's going to be 'Johnny Hustle.'"

Machado said exactly that, to Ken Rosenthal of The Athletic, in the middle of the 2018 National League Championship Series. With his team fighting for a World Series. Just a few weeks before he would hit the free agent market for the first time in his career.

On the one hand, Machado had become one of the best talents in the game. On the other, he'd become a player who was... proud of not hustling?

Machado went on to say he realizes it looks bad when he doesn't run hard on a ground ball, or when he has to stop at first base on what should have been a double because he dogged it out of the box.

"I look back at the video and I'm like, 'Woah, what am I doing?'" he told Rosenthal.

Realizing (or being told) his comments sounded bad, Machado later tried to retreat in an interview with MLB.com.

"When I was asked that question, I was definitely on the defensive, and I was wrong to answer it the way that I did, because looking back, it doesn't come across how I meant it," Machado said. "For me, I was trying to talk about how I'm not the guy who is eye wash. There's a difference between fake hustle for show and being someone who tries hard to win. I've always been the guy who does whatever he can to win for his team."

The damage control didn't sound very convincing, not when people saw what they saw in the playoffs.

Machado is hardly the only player in the big leagues who doesn't run out every ball. But it's still true that every manager will say he expects his team to play hard above all else, and that effort is one thing you can always bring to a game.

It's beyond just being an unwritten rule, because it isn't something that has changed or will change. You hit the ball and you run, and you do it every time if you want to be someone who is talked about as playing the game right.

It's why Hall of Famer Jim Palmer reacted so strongly to Machado not running.

"Once again Manny doesn't run hard," Palmer tweeted during the NLCS. "Down 1–0 in series, 0–0 game in 4th. Too tired to run hard for 90 feet. But wants the big $$ #pathetic."

It was quite a postseason for Machado, who was also called for an illegal slide into second base, handing the Brewers a double play, and twice kicked the first baseman's foot while crossing the bag.

Oh, and he hit .182 with a .390 OPS in the World Series, which his Los Angeles Dodgers lost to the Boston Red Sox. A website called The Baseball Gauge calculated a stat called championship win probability added, which tried to look at how each at-bat during the postseason affected a team's chances of winning the World Series. Machado, for what it's worth, ranked 238th among the 240 players, ahead of only Milwaukee Brewers reliever Jeremy Jeffress and Dodgers infielder/outfielder Enrique Hernandez.

Beyond not getting big hits, Machado seemed to be in the news constantly for doing something wrong. Major League Baseball fined him $10,000 for kicking the back of Brewers first baseman Jesus Aguilar's foot during the NLCS. Aguilar left his foot on the bag longer than necessary after taking a throw from shortstop on a Machado ground ball, but it was hard to understand why Machado would kick out at him while going past.

"It's a dirty play," Brewers outfielder Christian Yelich told reporters that night. "It's a dirty play by a dirty player."

And yet, a week later, Machado stepped on the foot of Boston Red Sox first baseman Steve Pearce in a similar-looking play in the World Series. The Pearce play clearly seemed unintentional, and Pearce brushed it aside by telling reporters he "barely felt it."

Machado said he and Pearce are "kind of, almost best friends," but it was yet another play that left Machado in a bad light.

"Hey Machado, step on Derrek Lee's heel like that and see what happens," former major league infielder Ryan Theriot posted on Twitter.

The Aguilar and Pearce plays will stick with Machado, just as A-Rod will always have the play from the 2004 American League Championship Series where he tried to slap the ball out of Red Sox pitcher Bronson Arroyo's glove. On that play, where Rodriguez was trying to avoid making an out at first base, he was instead called out for interference. He'd violated baseball etiquette, but he had also violated baseball rules.

Machado was already out on his two plays at first base. He was also out on the ground ball to short that ended the fourth inning of Game 2 of the NLCS in Milwaukee.

"Deep in the hole... long throw... Machado's not running," Joe Buck said on the Fox broadcast. "[Orlando] Arcia made the play, had to double-clutch... and Machado didn't hustle."

No, he's definitely not "Johnny Hustle."

And that breaks one of the most important unwritten rules of all.

30

Deception Is (Sometimes) Part of the Game

THERE'S NOTHING WRONG WITH THE HIDDEN BALL TRICK, unless you're the one that gets caught by it. Even then, it's your fault for not paying attention.

It's not against the rules. It's not against the unwritten rules.

Some forms of deception are. There's an entire section on balks, which in many cases are basically attempts by the pitcher to deceive a baserunner.

"The purpose of the balk rule is to prevent the pitcher from deliberately deceiving the baserunner." It says so right there in the rules. It's under Rule 6.02(a) Comment (Rule 8.05 Comment). It couldn't be clearer.

You can't deceive the baserunner. Except when you can. The balk rule applies to pitchers, and it applies to the way the pitcher delivers the ball to the plate or throws to a base. It doesn't apply to what Blue Jays shortstop Ryan Goins did to Yankees baserunner Todd Frazier in September 2017 at Rogers Centre.

Frazier was on second base when Jacoby Ellsbury flied out to right field for the second out of the third inning. Jays right fielder Jose Bautista threw the ball in to Goins, who was standing right next to Frazier at second base. With Frazier looking the other way, Goins faked throwing the ball back to the pitcher. When Frazier stepped off the base, Goins tagged him and the inning was over.

Frazier didn't complain. He understood it wasn't Goins who had done anything wrong. It was him.

"It's a bonehead play by me, to be honest with you," the very honest Frazier told reporters. "I have to have a better mindset about what is going on in the game. It's not a good play on my part. It could have changed the game."

Not everyone who gets caught by a deke is so understanding. Former major-league second baseman Marty Barrett was a master at it, earning him the nickname "Dekemaster," but rival Doug DeCinces reportedly accused him of "Little League bullshit" after Barrett caught DeCinces asleep off second base in a 1985 game in Boston. The most surprising (and embarrassing) part about that play was it was the second time in a month Barrett had pulled the same trick on the Angels.

"I'm surprised [it worked], because [Angels manager] Gene Mauch is a real good baseball man," Barrett said. "[But] it could happen to our team, it could happen to me. As long as guys keep getting off base, it's going to work."

Matt Williams loved the hidden-ball trick when he played third base for the Giants, Indians, and Diamondbacks. In one game in 1994, Williams pulled it on Dodgers rookie Rafael Bournigal after Bournigal had reached third on a triple. Bournigal even admitted what happened after Williams pretended to give the ball to pitcher Dave Burba.

"He asked me to step off the bag so he could clean it," Bournigal told reporters. "You have no friends in this business."

There are other ways to deke runners that also work.

Take the play where a runner from first base is going on the pitch. The batter hits a fly ball, but the runner doesn't realize it. One of the middle infielders makes like he's fielding a ground ball, convincing the runner to slide. Meanwhile, the outfielder is making the catch and throwing back to first to double the runner up. You see it done with some regularity by veteran infielders, and it works a lot of the time.

It worked big-time in a slightly different way in one of the most famous World Series games ever, Game 7 in the 1991 Series between the Braves and the Twins. Lonnie Smith was on first base after a leadoff single in the eighth inning of a scoreless game. Terry Pendleton followed with a drive into the left-center field gap. It easily should have scored Smith and put the Braves ahead. But Smith fell for a deke by Twins second baseman Chuck Knoblauch and shortstop Greg Gagne. Knoblauch made as if he were fielding a ground ball, while Gagne went to second base as if to take the throw. A confused Smith stopped just past the bag at second, holding up just long enough that he was only able to advance to third base.

Given the reprieve, Twins starter Jack Morris got out of the inning with the game still scoreless. Morris never did allow a run, going all 10 innings before the Twins won the game and the World Series on Gene Larkin's single in the bottom of the 10th.

What Knoblauch and Gagne did violated no rule, not a written one and not an unwritten one. It's embarrassing for a player who falls for it, but nobody gets hurt. Except when someone does.

It happened to Gene Clines of the Pirates way back in July 1973. He was going on a pitch that ended up being called ball four. Derrel Thomas of the Padres faked a tag, forcing Clines into a late slide. Clines hurt his ankle on the play and was out of the lineup for the next few weeks.

Something similar happened to Bryce Harper in September 2016. Harper was heading to third base on a triple when he saw Pirates infielder Jung Ho Kang make as if he was about to put down a tag. The throw had actually gone over Kang's head, and he figured the fake tag might keep Harper from scoring on the play. What it actually did was force Harper into an awkward late slide, one that cost him a jammed left thumb.

Not surprisingly, the Nationals threw at Kang the next time he came to the plate, leading to a brawl.

Other attempts to deceive the runner are fine. Outfielders can put their glove up to act as if they think they're going to catch a fly ball, even when they know they have no choice but to play it on a hop. If the baserunner holds up and doesn't get an extra base, that's on him—and it's to the credit of the outfielder. Same goes for the play Manny Machado made for the Orioles when he had just come up to the big leagues at age 20. Machado, playing third base, fielded a slow roller and realized he wouldn't have a play at first base. He also knew there was a runner behind him who had just reached (and rounded) third base. Smartly, Machado fielded the ball and faked a throw to first, before wheeling and throwing back to third to get the runner.

There's no doubt Machado deceived the runner with the play. There's also no doubt what he did was legal under baseball rules—and under the unwritten rules.

So what about what Alex Rodriguez did in May 2007 against the Blue Jays? You may remember it. Howie Clark certainly does.

Clark was the Blue Jays third baseman that day. He was standing near the base, ready to catch a pop fly, when Rodriguez, the Yankees baserunner, ran right behind him. As he ran past, A-Rod decided to distract Clark by yelling something. A-Rod later said he yelled, "Ha!"

Clark, thinking he must have heard shortstop John McDonald calling him off, backed away as the ball dropped. The inning continued, Jorge Posada (who hit the pop-up) got credit for a hit, and Jason Giambi followed with a two-run single.

Naturally, the Blue Jays weren't happy. McDonald had to be held back from trying to fight A-Rod. Manager John Gibbons had words with A-Rod. And Rodriguez just stood there smiling.

"Maybe I'm naive," Gibbons said after the game. "But to me, it's bush league. One thing, to everybody in this business, you always look at the Yankees and they do things right. They play hard, class operation, that's what the Yanks are known for. That's not Yankee baseball."

He's right. The umpires may have ruled Rodriguez violated no written rule, but he certainly violated the unwritten rules.

31

Is It Okay to Steal
(and We're Not Talking Bases)?

SO WHAT ABOUT SIGN-STEALING?

It's been going on for as long as baseball has been played. Hall of Famer Hank Greenberg, who played in the 1930s and '40s, said later that his Tigers manager Del Baker would steal catchers' signs while standing in the third-base coaching box. In the book *The Glory of Their Times*, Greenberg said Baker would yell "Alright, Hank, you can do it," if the next pitch was going to be a fastball, and "Come on, Hank, you can do it," if it was going to be a curve. With Baker as his manager in 1940, Greenberg drove in 150 runs.

Years after the famous Bobby Thomson "Shot heard 'round the world" in 1951, it came out that the New York Giants had been stealing signs that season, including during that historic playoff series against the Brooklyn Dodgers.

There's always been grumbling that the Chicago White Sox were stealing signs at Comiskey Park, or that the Toronto Blue

Jays were doing it at the Rogers Centre (or the SkyDome, as it was first known).

Then there was the controversy in 2017, the one that added a little juice to the rivalry between the New York Yankees and Boston Red Sox. It was revealed in a story early that September in the *New York Times*.

The Red Sox had come up with a sign-stealing scheme that involved using an Apple Watch in the dugout. Someone in their video room would figure out what sign sequence the Yankees catcher was using with a runner on second base, and he would relay it to a trainer in the dugout via the Apple Watch. The trainer would give it to the players, and the runner on second base would be able to read the signs and signal the hitter.

One problem: the Yankees saw them doing it, videotaped it, and reported it to the commissioner's office. And then somebody told the *Times*.

The New York tabloids loved it.

"Dirty Sox," the *Daily News* screamed.

"Boston Cheat Party," said the *Post*. For the rest of the season, the *Post* put an asterisk next to Boston in the American League East standings; "*caught stealing," it read.

Using technology or cameras to help with stealing signs is against baseball's written rules, and while the Red Sox weren't seriously punished—they were only fined, because baseball decided the front-office wasn't aware of the scheme—they were told to stop doing it.

The Houston Astros weren't fined during the 2018 playoffs, even though they had an employee pointing a camera into the

Red Sox dugout. The Astros claimed they were trying to make sure the Red Sox weren't cheating, perhaps by using an unauthorized iPad or other technology. The Astros employee was told to leave the area and stop filming, but MLB accepted the explanation.

"I think it's really important to think through what the rules are, okay?" commissioner Rob Manfred told reporters. "Sign stealing in and of itself is not a violation of our rules. It's been a part of our game since Lassie was a puppy. Where it becomes a problem is where there is a use of technology that otherwise violates our rules to aid the sign-stealing process."

Technology has become more ever-present in baseball, just as in any other part of life. Teams have more cameras available for evaluation, and each team has a video room to help decide whether or not to challenge an umpire's call. None of those are supposed to be used to help decipher signs, however.

As Manfred said, sign-stealing itself doesn't violate rules, written or unwritten. When the Red Sox discovered the Dodgers' Manny Machado relaying signs to his batters from second base, they were upset with themselves for not dealing with it, and not with Machado for stealing the signs.

"Oh, it's clean," Red Sox pitching coach Dana LeVangie told Scott Miller of Bleacher Report. "It's baseball. If you're not hiding your stuff with a runner on second base and you're giving them a free view, that's on you, the pitcher, and the catcher. It's up to the pitcher and catcher to manage that and to us to oversee it and make sure we're going about it the right way."

In fact, most players or teams would tell you the responsibility is on the team giving the signs. They need to protect themselves, and they need to be aware and change the signs if necessary.

Teams are aware, more than ever. It was once unusual for catchers to give complicated signs to a pitcher unless there was a runner on second base (where he could obviously see the signs). Now it's routine for catchers to use complex sequences even without a runner on second. LeVangie said Red Sox pitchers and catchers typically change their signs every pitch.

All of that slows down the game, which is one reason many people have suggested baseball adopt an NFL-style in-helmet communication system that would allow the catcher to simply tell the pitcher what he wants the next pitch to be.

Smart players and coaches look for anything that tips them off to what pitch is coming next, whether it's a sign they can see or a pitcher who does something different depending on what he's about to throw. Same thing goes for signs the third-base coach gives to the batters and baserunners, or to signals coming from the dugout. Longtime major league coach Joe Nossek was considered a master at deciphering signs.

In the case of the "Shot heard 'round the world," the Giants were using more than just their eyes. It didn't come out until years later. A writer named Joshua Prager came up with it and put it first in the *Wall Street Journal* and later in a book called *The Echoing Green*.

At the Polo Grounds, the clubhouses were in center field (in modern ballparks, they're behind the dugouts). Giants manager Leo Durocher had coach Herman Franks sit in the Giants clubhouse with a telescope during games. Franks could clearly see the signs the catcher put down, and he had access to an electric buzzer system that connected to the Giants bullpen in deep right field. The pitchers in the bullpen could then signal the pitch to the batters.

Teams that don't do a good enough job of protecting their signs—or those who are just paranoid—have been complaining about it for as long as sign-stealing has been going on.

The key is not getting caught. In the old days, that was a good way to wear one, as in getting a fastball to the ribs. Now you might end up starting a fight.

The only problem the Red Sox had was that the Yankees saw them using the Apple Watch in the dugout. That's against baseball rules. But there are plenty of ways around it, ways where you can get the information where it needs to get without anyone seeing that you're doing it.

With more and more technology available, teams are going to use it in many ways to gain an edge. They should. It's the other team's responsibility to protect the integrity of their own signs.

It's easy to become paranoid. In 2011, ESPN ran a report with American League players accusing the Blue Jays of relaying signs at Rogers Centre, via a man dressed in white in the outfield seats. Three years later, Chris Sale (then with the White Sox) accused the Tigers of using binoculars to steal signs from beyond the center-field fence at Comerica Park.

Schemes like that violate baseball rules, but the key is catching them in time to do something about it. Giving more complex signs is one way to do it, but that can also have a side-effect of slowing the pitcher's rhythm. Not only that but it increases the risk the pitcher misreads or forgets the sequence and crosses the catcher up, risking a wild pitch or passed ball.

But there are other ways to do it.

The simplest one is for the pitcher and catcher to set things up before an inning, and for the catcher to signal a breaking ball and have the pitcher throw a fastball up and in instead. It should only take one time, one fastball sailing in to a hitter diving over the plate to hit the down-and-away slider he's expecting.

That batter won't want anyone giving him the pitches again.

32

It's Only Cheating
If You Get Caught

THERE'S A FAMOUS STORY LOU PINIELLA TELLS ABOUT THE time George Steinbrenner called him in the dugout during a game. Piniella was managing the Yankees, and Steinbrenner was watching the game on television. The Yankees were playing in Anaheim, and the TV announcers said it looked like Angels pitcher Don Sutton was doctoring the ball. Steinbrenner told Piniella he wasn't doing his job, and why hadn't he gotten the umpires to stop Sutton from cheating.

The way Piniella described it to Jerome Holtzman of the *Chicago Tribune* a few years later, he let Steinbrenner talk for a while before asking him who was winning the game. The Yankees were. And who was pitching for the Yankees? Tommy John.

"Who do you think taught Sutton how to cheat?" Piniella asked. "It was Tommy John. And if I go out and bother Sutton they'll undress our guy on the mound."

Sutton went seven innings that day and allowed just three hits. But John pitched just as well. The Yankees won the game in 11 innings.

There's a lesson there, one that helps keep cheating alive in the game. Be careful accusing an opponent if your guy might be doing the same thing.

It's not nearly as much of an issue in the modern game, simply because not many pitchers even know what to do with a scuffed baseball. Watch them toss a ball out of play when it comes back to them with any kind of mark. Old-time pitchers see that and can't believe it, because they would love the chance to make that ball dance on the next pitch.

Many of those old-time pitchers would find a way to hide sandpaper or Vaseline, or they'd have a catcher or an infielder put a convenient cut on a ball before returning it to the mound.

Every now and then, someone got caught. Brian Moehler got caught with sandpaper in 1999. Joe Niekro got caught with an emery board and sandpaper in 1987. Kevin Gross got caught with sandpaper, also in 1987. Rick Honeycutt got caught with a thumbtack in 1980.

And in 2014, Michael Pineda of the Yankees was suspended because he had tons of pine tar on his neck while pitching an April game in Boston.

Four years later, baseball had another mini-controversy involving pine tar. Trevor Bauer of the Cleveland Indians took to Twitter in May 2018 and accused other pitchers of using the substance to increase spin rate. The implication was that the Houston Astros were cheating, and that Bauer's UCLA teammate and rival, Gerrit Cole, was taking advantage of it. (Cole's spin rate rose in his first season after going to the Astros in a trade with the Pittsburgh Pirates.)

The Astros accused Bauer of jealousy. Bauer accused Major League Baseball of enforcing the rules selectively.

And nobody ever really agreed whether pitchers using pine tar—especially in cold weather early and late in the season—was a good or bad idea.

Many managers and hitters said they were in favor of anything that would allow a pitcher to get a better grip on the ball.

"Absolutely," Washington Nationals outfielder Bryce Harper told Bleacher Report. "I'm all for it. If there's a guy out there that needs it, I'm all for it. I don't want to get hit in the head or the face. So whatever they need out there, I'll let them have it."

Other hitters didn't agree.

"I consider it cheating," New York Mets third baseman Todd Frazier said. "Anything to help somebody out, whether it's getting grip on the ball or whatever it is. They'll come out and say, 'You need grip on your bat.' Yeah, we do, but the grip part isn't on the barrel of the bat where we hit. And when it is, you'll get caught."

In the end, nothing happened. Nothing changed. The controversy blew over, at least until the next time someone accuses a pitcher of using pine tar to gain an advantage.

This is one case where the unwritten rules go against the rules that are in the book. The written rules say a pitcher can't "apply a foreign substance of any kind to the ball," or "deface the ball in any manner."

The unwritten rules say you just can't make it too obvious or too over the top. That's what Pineda did, and that's why Red Sox manager John Farrell felt he had no choice but to talk to the umpires about it. The umpires at that point had no choice but to throw Pineda out of the game, and MLB had no choice but to suspend him (for 10 games, as it turned out).

Baseballs right out of the box are too slick to grip. Before every game, clubhouse attendants rub them up with a special kind of mud. But any pitcher will tell you that in cold weather even a rubbed-up ball will feel so slick in your hands that you can't grip it.

That's a problem for a pitcher, but if the pitcher is throwing 100 mph and doesn't know where it's going, it can quickly become a problem for a hitter, too. So most hitters want the pitcher to be able to get a grip—but that opens up the possibility of using a substance that mimics the old spitball. Pitchers have been known to use a combination of rosin, sunscreen, and pine tar. Pitchers have taken the mound with what seems like too much gel in their hair, or too much pine tar on their caps.

Pineda wasn't the first pitcher to get caught with pine tar, and he wasn't the first to get suspended. Julian Tavarez of the Cardinals had pine tar on his cap in 2004, and he got 10 games, too. So did Brendan Donnelly of the Angels, caught with pine tar on his glove a year later. Joel Peralta of the Rays had pine tar on his glove in 2012, and he was suspended when Nationals manager Davey Johnson asked the umpires to check him.

How did Johnson know about Peralta's glove? Simple. Peralta had pitched for the Nationals two years before. Rays manager

Joe Maddon claimed that using that prior knowledge was "underhanded" and "a form of cheating." Johnson shot back that Maddon was a "weird wuss," and that he ought to read the rule book.

The unwritten rule book says Peralta didn't do anything wrong. He didn't even make the pine tar obvious, as Kenny Rogers of the Tigers did when he took the mound at Comerica Park for Game 2 of the 2006 World Series. In the first inning that night, the Fox TV cameras closed in on Rogers' pitching hand, which appeared to be doused in pine tar.

The umpires that night didn't throw Rogers out of the game. They did talk to both managers, and before Rogers took the mound for the second inning, he seemed to have washed his hand.

Rogers ended up throwing a shutout that night, so perhaps Cardinals manager Tony La Russa should have put up a bigger fuss. Or maybe he was doing just as Piniella did that day when Steinbrenner called.

Maybe he knew the Cardinals pitchers were using pine tar, too.

33

Can We Say "No-Hitter?"

ENOUGH WITH THE TALK OF CHEATING OR STEALING OR trying to get away with something you may not have earned. It's time to move on to something a pitcher has earned, by getting deep into a game without giving up a hit.

What he's earned is a seat in the dugout with plenty of space all around him, the entire time his team is batting.

You don't talk to a pitcher when he's throwing a no-hitter. Is there any bigger taboo in baseball than that? We're really talking about a pitcher who might be throwing a no-hitter, because until he gets 27 outs you don't know whether this is the game that's going to end up being special. Until the starting pitcher has allowed a hit, though, there's a chance it might be.

There's a point in the game where it begins to matter that he hasn't yet allowed a hit. It's not that hard to tell when it is. Just watch the starter when the camera shows him in the dugout between innings.

Is anyone talking to him?

It's funny, because you'll hear some pitchers who have thrown no-hitters say they wanted someone to talk to. But etiquette is etiquette, and nobody's going to be the guy who gets blamed for messing up someone's no-hit bid.

The unwritten rule on this one is pretty simple: if a guy's got a no-hitter going, you don't talk to him.

It's not like guys talk much to the starting pitcher during any game. Every pitcher's personality is different, but most of them are pretty locked in on the days they pitch. They don't want much unnecessary conversation before the games, and they don't want it between innings, either. They're focused on the job, thinking about the next hitters coming up and what they need to do to get them out.

But there's always been that thing about a no-hitter, about how nobody in the dugout should even mention the words for fear of jinxing it. Some announcers and fans even think that should apply to them, although it's pretty clear it doesn't. The great Vin Scully never hesitated to tell his listeners that the pitcher (for the Dodgers or the opponent) hadn't allowed a hit, and he called plenty of no-hitters. Jon Miller with the Giants and Gary Cohen with the Mets don't believe their words can affect what happens on the field, and they've both called no-hitters, too.

Meanwhile, plenty of announcers who have tied themselves in knots trying to avoid saying the words "no-hitter" have watched one no-hit bid after another get broken up. Oh well. Someone else must have jinxed it, right?

In reality, the players not involved in the game don't have any impact on what happens, either, but that doesn't mean they can't be superstitious. When F.P. Santangelo screams "same seats!" to listeners of his Washington Nationals telecasts he's just doing the same thing guys sitting in the bullpen or the clubhouse are doing during a no-hit bid or a rally. No one moves. Everyone does the same thing they were doing all along.

And no one has any unnecessary words for the guy trying to throw the no-hitter.

In the book he did with Tim Brown, *Imperfect: An Improbable Life*, Jim Abbott said he noticed it after the sixth inning of his 1993 no-hitter.

"Teammates who might have mentioned a pitch here or there, grunted something about a good or crummy play, commented on another score in another town, began to keep those observations to themselves," Abbott said.

David Cone, who liked talking to anyone before and during his 419 starts in the big leagues, remembered years after his 1999 perfect game that only Chili Davis would talk to him during that game.

"I would walk up to the clubhouse in the locker room in between innings and change my undershirt—the little routine that I had—even the clubhouse kids, anybody in there, just left," Cone told the *New York Post* years later. "So I had the whole clubhouse to myself."

Cone did get the perfect game, so maybe it worked.

A little more than a year before Cone threw his perfect game, David Wells threw one for the Yankees against the Minnesota Twins. Cone played a part in that one, too.

Wells' other teammates began avoiding him as the game went on. At one point, Wells sat down next to Darryl Strawberry, and Strawberry got up and walked away. No one wanted to take a chance on being the guy who jinxed it.

No one except Cone.

Cone and Wells were already good friends, and Cone understood better than most that what Wells really needed was someone saying something to take his mind off the pressure of not having allowed a baserunner. So as the Yankees were batting in the seventh inning, adding their two final runs to make it a 4–0 game, Cone started talking.

"I think it's time to break out the knuckleball," he said.

Wells, of course, doesn't throw a knuckleball. But he did enjoy the interlude.

Twenty years after the perfect game, thinking back on it, he could only recite three of the outs.

"That's all I remember, besides David Cone yelling at me," Wells said.

He did remember his feelings as the ninth inning began.

"You're a mess," he said. "Your stomach's turning. You're nervous as hell. You're thinking, 'Don't make a mistake.' That's exactly what I was saying to myself."

The unwritten rule on not talking to a guy throwing a no-hitter is so established that some players get uncomfortable even if it's the pitcher initiating the conversation. When Giants rookie Chris Heston no-hit the Mets in 2015, Heston made an eighth-inning baserunning mistake that cost teammate Matt Duffy a run. In the top of the ninth, Heston went over to Duffy to apologize. Duffy was stunned.

"After the sixth, I didn't want to go anywhere within five feet of him," Duffy told Andrew Baggarly of the *San Jose Mercury News*. "We were in the dugout right before the ninth and he said, 'Hey man, I'm sorry about that.' I said, 'Dude, uh, don't worry about it. Don't focus on that. It's fine.'"

Heston must not have worried too much. He got the no-hitter.

Sonny Gray, on the other hand, did not get a no-hitter on Opening Day 2015. He carried it to the eighth inning, but Ryan Rua led off with a base hit. It probably wasn't because Gray had talked to manager Bob Melvin in the dugout, but then again, why did Gray tempt fate by asking Melvin about his new warmup song?

"Get away from me," Melvin said later, relaying what he told Gray in the dugout. "No one wants to talk about walk-up songs. No one wants to talk to you right now."

34

Can You Bunt for the First Hit?

SO YOU DON'T TALK TO A PITCHER WHO MIGHT BE throwing a no-hitter. And the manager is hesitant to take out a pitcher who still hasn't allowed a hit (although pitch counts can now force his hand). You'll also hear some official scorers who still maintain the first hit should be a clean one, and that anything close is an error.

That last one really shouldn't be. A hit is a hit. What, should an umpire err on the side of calling the batter out if it's a close play at first, or if it's a third strike just on (or off) the black?

But what about bunting? Is it alright to bunt for the first hit?

That depends.

Tradition says you don't. Do it against the wrong pitcher in the old days and you were likely to get a fastball in the back (or an even worse spot) the next time up.

Like so many other things, it's much more complicated now. It's more or less accepted that bunting is fine if the goal is to win the game rather than simply to deny the pitcher his shot at history. If it's a close game, your team needs baserunners, and bunting for a hit is part of your game, go right ahead. If it's 7–0 with two out in the eighth, that might not be the best spot for it.

The new wrinkle in the modern game is the shift. If the defensive team is still shifting and leaving the third-base line wide open, is it really against any unwritten rule for the batter to bunt?

That exact situation came up in a September 2014 game between the San Diego Padres and Philadelphia Phillies. Padres starter Andrew Cashner hadn't allowed a hit when Domonic Brown came to the plate with one out in the fifth. Brown bats left-handed, and the Padres set up their shift with three infielders on the right side. And Brown bunted for the first hit of the game.

The fans at Petco Park booed Brown. Cashner stared at him.

"You can ask him what I thought of it," Cashner told reporters after the game.

But Padres manager Bud Black wasn't complaining. Black noted that it was a close game. The Padres led 1–0, which would also end up being the final score.

"There was more grumbling in the stands than in the dugout [about the bunt]," Black said. "Our defensive metrics say we're going to shift on this fellow. He's playing the game."

The same thing happened in 2012, with the A's playing the Red Sox. Oakland's A.J. Griffin had a perfect game going in the fifth inning. But with the A's shifting on Jarrod Saltalamacchia, Saltalamacchia bunted for the game's first hit.

"I probably should have had the third baseman in," A's manager Bob Melvin admitted.

Not every pitcher gets upset when a bunt is the first hit, especially when it comes from a speedster like Jarrod Dyson. Dyson is so fast his Twitter handle is @mrzoombiya.

"Hey, that's what I do," Dyson explained to Bob Dutton of the *Kansas City Star* in 2013. "I zoom by you."

Four years later, in June 2017, Dyson was playing for the Mariners, and Justin Verlander was bidding for a perfect game for the Detroit Tigers. At least he was until Dyson bunted for a hit with one out in the sixth inning of a game the Tigers led, 4–0.

"It was a perfect bunt," Verlander said. "That's part of his game. I don't think it was quite too late in the game given the situation to bunt, especially being how it's a major part of what he does. So I didn't really have any issues with it. It wasn't like I got upset about it."

Verlander was more upset that Dyson's bunt single started a three-run rally in a game the Mariners came back to win, 7–5.

Bunting is definitely a part of Dyson's game. By the end of 2017, he had 46 bunt hits in his career. Compare that to Ben Davis. He may have never bunted for a hit, except for one game in 2001. He was playing for the Padres against the Diamondbacks that day, it was in the eighth inning, and D-Backs pitcher Curt Schilling still hadn't allowed a hit. Davis bunted with two out and nobody on, and he reached base with the Padres' first hit. The Diamondbacks weren't happy. Manager Bob Brenly yelled at Davis as he stood at first base, and later called Davis "chickenshit."

"I know there's two schools of thought on it," Brenly told reporters a few days later. "One, they're trying to get the tying run to the plate to win a ballgame [the Diamondbacks led 2–0 at the time]. I can certainly understand that, but the way I was raised in this game, the guys who taught me how to play the game when I was coming up taught me there's a certain respect for the game, respect for the opponents, especially when they're doing something exceptional. And there's no question that's what Curt was doing."

The only problem with what Brenly said is that respect for the game means trying to win, and by bunting for a hit, Davis brought the tying run to the plate. Why should it be on him to help Schilling do "something exceptional?" Schilling would pitch out of the inning and end up with a complete-game three-hitter and a win, but at the time the Padres needed a baserunner to have a chance.

"I don't think anyone should tell us to drop our weapons and raise our hands," Padres manager Bruce Bochy said. "Ben did the right thing.

Brenly wasn't convinced.

"They're sure they're right, and we're sure we're right," he said. "I don't know if there is a right or wrong."

Years later, Davis told Todd Zolecki of MLB.com he had no idea why anyone would be upset with him. He said he went up to teammate Tony Gwynn and asked if he'd done something wrong.

"Man, forget those guys," Gwynn told him, according to Davis. "You did nothing wrong."

Bunting can cause issues even when a no-hitter isn't at stake.

On the final day of August 2017 at Yankee Stadium, Eduardo Nunez of the Red Sox bunted for a hit in the first inning against

Yankee starter CC Sabathia. Sabathia didn't like it, and he let everyone know he didn't like it.

"It's kind of weak to me," he said after the game, after cursing toward the Red Sox dugout on his way off the field at the end of the inning. "I'm an old man. They should go out there and try to kick my butt."

The problem with that is there's no rule against bunting for a hit, and no unwritten rule against it, either. There's absolutely nothing there suggesting teams can't bunt for hits when the pitcher is 37 years old, has bad knees, and is overweight.

Teams aren't going to stop running because the pitcher can't hold runners on or the catcher has a weak arm. Pitchers aren't going to stop throwing curveballs because the batter can't hit them.

Teams tried bunting on Jim Abbott, who was born without a right hand and had to shift his glove to his left hand, his pitching hand, after delivering the ball to the plate. To be able to pitch in the big leagues, Abbott had to show he could handle it, that bunting on him wasn't going to be a successful strategy.

CC can handle bunts, too. If he couldn't, he wouldn't have lasted 18 years in the major leagues. If teams could beat him by bunting on him, they'd be doing it regularly. As it was, there were only seven successful bunt hits off him in 148.2 innings in 2017, according to Fangraphs. That was the most in the major leagues, but it was hardly an outrageous total. Drew Pomeranz allowed nine bunt hits in 2016, and Jered Weaver allowed 10 in 2014.

In 153 innings in 2018, Sabathia allowed just two bunt hits.

The Fangraphs numbers don't go back far enough to tell us how many guys bunted successfully off Nolan Ryan. What we do know is that Ryan didn't like it any better than Sabathia does. But instead of just complaining, Ryan would do something about it.

"I can remember the first time I faced Nolan Ryan," Brett Butler, an outfielder who liked to bunt, told Boston's WBUR radio in 2016. "And there's a guy, a Hall of Famer that threw almost 100. I remember squaring around and taking a pitch—kind of gauging and seeing what was going on—and he yelled at me from the mound, 'Swing the bat! Swing the bat or I'm going to hit you right in the head.' Well, again, there's intimidation involved in that. But the reason Nolan did that is that Nolan didn't like to field the bunt."

It wasn't an idle threat, either. Ryan would throw at a guy who bunted. He might not actually hit him in the head, but he might try to take out his legs. He was willing to put that guy on base to make his point, counting on the pain as a message not to try to bunt the next time.

Pitchers today don't do that. Sabathia doesn't, and he might not want anyone else to, either. His teammate, Brett Gardner, had 51 career bunt hits through the end of 2018, again according to Fangraphs. Some of those hits, no doubt, have helped Sabathia win a game. You can bet Gardner chooses carefully when he's going to attempt a bunt. You can bet he's more likely to try it if the guy on the mound, or the first baseman or third baseman, has shown to be a little weaker fielding them.

When CC complained about Nunez's bunt hit, and also about a similar attempt by Andrew Benintendi a couple of weeks before at Fenway Park, former Red Sox slugger Jim Rice hauled off on him on Boston's NESN TV channel.

"What is he talking about? Bunting is part of the game," Rice said on the Red Sox' postgame show. "You try to get on the base any way you can. If you tell him to leave some of that chicken, that doughnut, and that burger weight, maybe his leg will be okay, that he can field that baseball. That's just stupid."

Even CC seemed to get a kick out of those comments, at least after he called Rice "bitter."

"It's just funny," he said. "He's right. I'm fat. He won that."

For the record, Sabathia won both those games where the Red Sox tried to bunt on him. Maybe he should have asked them to bunt more.

Speaking of which, the Sabathia comments reminded some people of another game and another pitcher who might have had trouble moving off the mound. Remember Game 6 of the 2004 ALCS, when Schilling beat the Yankees while pitching after surgery on his ankle? Remember the TV cameras zooming in on Schilling's right foot and ankle, showing what seemed to be blood seeping through his sock?

Schilling pitched seven innings that night at old Yankee Stadium. He gave up four hits. Not one of them was a bunt. The Yankees never tried. Yankees manager Joe Torre didn't even put Kenny Lofton in the lineup that night, even though Lofton was a good enough bunter that he once had 15 bunt hits in a season.

Three years later, as some in New York are happy to point out, Lofton did try to bunt in the playoffs. By that time, Lofton was playing for the Indians, and he bunted against Roger Clemens, a

45-year-old pitcher with hamstring trouble. Clemens aggravated the hamstring trying to field the bunt, in what turned out to be the last major league game Clemens ever pitched.

Clemens and the Yankees didn't complain about Lofton trying to bunt. They understood it was part of his game, and part of the game of baseball.

There's nothing in the rules against it. Not in the written rules, and not in the unwritten rules, either.

Except, sometimes, when the pitcher hasn't yet allowed a hit.

35

You Don't Pull a Pitcher
Before He Allows a Hit
(Unless You Do)

NOLAN RYAN, AS MOST BASEBALL FANS KNOW, THREW
seven no-hitters in his Hall of Fame career. No one else has
thrown more than four. What most fans don't know is that Ryan
actually started 15 games in which he didn't give up a hit. There
were six games when he left early because of injuries, and a
game in 1976 when he wasn't even supposed to start but faced
one batter because Angels manager Dick Williams mistakenly
put him on the lineup card.

The pitcher on the card had to face one batter before he
could be removed, so Ryan took the mound at Comiskey Park,
threw two pitches and got Chet Lemon to ground out before
Williams replaced him with Gary Ross, who was supposed to
start that day.

"I definitely had my no-hit stuff," Ryan joked to reporters after
the game.

And then there was the game on April 9, 1990, the one and
only time a manager chose to pull Nolan Ryan from a game

when he was pitching a no-hitter. Even then, there were special circumstances. The owners had locked out the players in a labor dispute that wasn't settled until March 19. Spring training lasted only two weeks. So after Ryan threw 91 pitches in five innings on Opening Day, Rangers manager Bobby Valentine decided that was enough.

"I was hoping for rain and a five-inning complete game," Valentine explained afterwards. "I even called the weather report and if it was going to rain before 10 o'clock, I was going to send him back out there."

But there was no rain. Ryan, who was 43 years old at the time, admitted to reporters that night he was exhausted and couldn't have finished the game.

That's what it took to get Nolan Ryan out of a game when he hadn't allowed a hit. Nowadays, with almost every pitcher and almost any manager, it takes much less. Four times in the 2017 season alone, a manager pulled a starter who hadn't allowed a hit (and wasn't hurt). It happened five times in 2016, with Dodgers manager Dave Roberts pulling Rich Hill after seven perfect innings.

"I'm going to lose sleep tonight," Roberts said. "And I probably should."

It's happening to managers more and more often. By the 2018 All-Star break, there had already been seven games where a pitcher threw six no-hit innings and didn't go any further.

In the case of Julio Teheran of the Atlanta Braves, it was a hamstring cramp that combined with his high pitch count (95 through six innings) to force him from the game. Nathan

Eovaldi was making his first start back in the big leagues after recovering from a second Tommy John surgery when Tampa Bay Rays manager Kevin Cash told him six innings and 70 pitches were enough.

"He just kind of stared at me," Cash told reporters. "He wouldn't shake my hand."

But with the advent of pitch counts and the belief that throwing too many pitches risks injury, managers start doing math when their pitcher gets to the fifth or sixth inning without allowing a hit. Is the count at that point in the game low enough that he can realistically get through nine without getting to a number that is unacceptable.

Sean Newcomb of the Atlanta Braves had thrown 88 pitches in six no-hit innings in July 2018 against the Los Angeles Dodgers. Braves manager Brian Snitker sent Newcomb out for the seventh and then sent him out for the eighth with a pitch count at 100. Newcomb had never thrown more than 111 pitches in any of his previous 39 major-league starts, but Snitker allowed him to begin the ninth inning after he had already thrown 117 pitches.

Snitker had been in professional baseball for more than 40 years and between the minor leagues and the majors he had managed more than 3,000 games. But he was nervous in the ninth inning that day, just as he had been a year earlier when Braves pitcher Mike Foltynewicz lost a no-hit bid with just three outs to go.

Newcomb would get even closer, getting the first two outs of the ninth before Manny Machado's single denied him the no-hitter. By then, Newcomb had thrown 134 pitches, the most by any Braves pitcher since 2000.

"I stopped looking at the pitch count," said Snitker, who understood what a no-hitter would mean to his 25-year-old left-hander. "But it's like I told him after the game. When I was managing in Durham [in the 1980s], that [134 pitches] was just a normal game."

Not anymore. Newcomb was the only pitcher in the major leagues who threw as many as 130 pitches in a game in 2018. Compare that to 1989, when there were 198 times a pitcher threw 130 pitches in a game (and when Tommy Lasorda allowed Orel Hershiser to throw 169 in one game for the Dodgers).

Ten years later, the number of 130-pitch games had been cut nearly in half, to 103. By 2009, it had dropped to just seven games (with no pitcher throwing more than 133).

This is one case where the unwritten rules have changed drastically. Pitch counts have changed how managers handle their pitching in every game, but the decisions are toughest when the starter hasn't allowed a hit. Even the newest of new-age managers understands the value of making history, that throwing a no-hitter can change a pitcher's life. But every manager also understands that today's pitchers aren't conditioned to throw 120 pitches in a game.

As Roberts said when he pulled Ross Stripling after 100 pitches in 7⅓ no-hit innings in April 2016, "Under no circumstance am I going to even consider putting his future in jeopardy. For me, it was a no-brainer."

Accurate pitch counts have only been available for the last 30 years or so, so we don't know how many pitches Ryan threw in most of his no-hitters (he threw 130 and 122 in his last two). We do know Giants manager Bruce Bochy allowed Tim Lincecum to throw 148 pitches in a 2013 no-hitter, and A.J. Hinch allowed Edwin Jackson to throw 149 in his 2010 no-hitter for the Diamondbacks.

"He kept saying, 'I'm fine. I'm not coming out. I'm not coming out,'" Hinch said that night. "You do want to make smart decisions, but you do have a chance at history and you don't want to take it away from him."

It's understandable for managers to worry about putting pitchers' careers in jeopardy. Terry Collins agonized over allowing Johan Santana to throw 134 pitches in his 2012 no-hitter for the Mets. Santana, who was 33 years old at the time and had already had injury trouble, started only 10 more games in his major league career. There's no way to know if the 134-pitch game contributed, or how much it did.

"You can't say it was the right decision or the wrong decision," Santana told *Sports Illustrated* in 2015. "Maybe if I would have gotten knocked out in the fourth inning, everything would have been different, or nothing would have been different."

Collins said in that story that Mets fans tell him all the time they're glad he allowed Santana to continue. The Mets had never had a pitcher throw a no-hitter in their history, and through 2018 Santana's is still the only one they've ever had.

History is important, and not just to fans. Keeping pitchers healthy to have long careers is important to them and to the teams that invest money in them. It's easy to say you wouldn't pull a pitcher before he allowed his first hit, or to say you wouldn't let a pitcher go past a prescribed pitch limit.

It's not that easy, not anymore. The unwritten rule still says you don't pull a guy throwing a no-hitter—except when you do.

36

Starting Off with an Opener

THE TAMPA BAY RAYS HAVE HAD JUST ONE NO-HITTER IN
their history. Matt Garza threw it, on July 26, 2010, against the
Detroit Tigers.

Nine innings, 120 pitches, no hits.

Compare that to what Ryne Stanek did in eight of the games
he started for the Rays in 2018.

One and two-thirds innings, 21 pitches, no hits.

Two innings, 27 pitches, no hits.

One and two-thirds innings, 11 pitches, no hits.

One and two-thirds innings, 32 pitches, no hits.

One and two-thirds innings, 23 pitches, no hits.

Two innings, 22 pitches, no hits.

One inning, 16 pitches, no hits.

One out, 15 pitches, no hits.

Notice a difference?

The Rays actually had 15 games in 2018 where manager Kevin
Cash removed his pitcher before he'd allowed a hit. No manager

before him—and no other manager in 2018—had done it more than five times in a season.

In the past, it basically only happened when the pitcher got hurt or got ejected from the game, or when his pitch count was so high that the manager worried about the risk of injury. Cash and the Rays had a couple of cases like that, when he removed Nathan Eovaldi after six no-hit innings in his first start back after a second Tommy John surgery and when he pulled Blake Snell after five perfect innings in his second start after spending time on the disabled list with shoulder fatigue.

In all the other cases, Cash made a change because the pitcher who started the game wasn't really a starter. On those days, the Rays didn't even call their first pitcher a starter.

He was an opener, and there was no new piece of baseball strategy that led to more debates in 2018. By the end of the season, many teams had copied the Rays and tried it, and there was even discussion of whether it might be the best way to approach some playoff games.

The idea, in simplest terms, came out of the truth that more runs are scored in the first inning than in any other inning. So why not use a one-inning specialist as your first pitcher?

And once you've done that, why not think about having that pitcher work through the middle of the opposition batting order? You can even follow him, as the Rays sometimes did, with a pitcher expected to work the most innings of anyone you use that day, someone who in other cases would have been the starter. By using an opener before him, you could allow that other pitcher to begin his day's work in the lower part of the order.

The strategy was first suggested by MLB Network's Brian Kenny in his 2016 book, *Ahead of the Curve: Inside the Baseball Revolution*. The Rays didn't follow it fully, because Kenny suggested even using an opener in games where you have a pitcher like Clayton Kershaw available to pitch as many as seven innings.

The Rays didn't use an opener on days where they had what Cash called a "traditional starter," such as Blake Snell, Chris Archer, or Nathan Eovaldi before they traded them. Their original plan was to have four traditional starters and one "bullpen day" each turn through the rotation. But injuries and the trades of Archer and Eovaldi left them short of pitchers they trusted to start games.

By the middle of May, they went from "bullpen days," which wouldn't include anyone expected to pitch 3–4 innings, to the opener, where a reliever would start the game and generally be asked to face as few as three or as many as nine batters, before giving way to someone who would likely take the game into the middle or late innings.

They ended up using an opener 55 times, although Cash strongly suggested he would have preferred using the strategy a little less, if he had more traditional starters available.

That said, the results were good. The Rays' first-inning ERA was an American League-best 3.61 and their record in games without a traditional starter was 44–34 (including "bullpen days" and games started by an opener).

By the end of the 2018 season, several other teams were trying the same thing, sometimes even going beyond what the Rays had done.

The Milwaukee Brewers took the strategy to an extreme on September 24, 2018, against the St. Louis Cardinals. With a bullpen bolstered by September call-ups that gave him a 19-man pitching staff and a Cardinals lineup with dangerous left-handed hitter Matt Carpenter in the leadoff spot followed by eight straight right-handed hitters, Brewers manager Craig Counsell chose to start lefty reliever Dan Jennings as what the team termed its "initial out-getter."

That's "out," as in singular, because Jennings was charged with simply getting one out. He went to the mound to begin the game, but his one and only job was to pitch to Carpenter. He threw three pitchers, got Carpenter to ground out to second base, and his day was done.

"Somebody asked me before the game if I was going to go five tonight," Jennings said. "I said, 'Five pitches?'"

It was a strategy born of circumstance—a September bullpen, a left-handed hitter who fares significantly better against right-handed pitchers atop a lineup filled with right-handed hitters, and a young "starting" pitcher who wasn't in position to feel slighted by coming out of the bullpen one out into the first inning.

Counsell followed Jennings with 22-year-old Freddy Peralta, who got the next 11 outs while allowing one run on three hits. One of those hits was an RBI double in the third by Carpenter, which if anything strengthened Counsell's case for using an "initial out-getter" against the Cardinals star.

The Brewers won the game, using nine pitchers along the way.

The Brewers made it to the postseason in 2018 without any dominant starting pitchers but with a bullpen that ranked fifth in baseball with a 3.49 ERA. But the Jennings game was the only one in the regular season where they employed anything that could be called an opener.

Then came the playoffs, when the Brewers took the concept of a rotation and basically discarded it.

In Game 1 of the division series against the Colorado Rockies, Counsell used Brandon Woodruff as his first pitcher. Call him the starter, the opener, or the initial out-getter, but understand that in that game, Woodruff's job would be to face only the first nine batters.

It didn't matter that he got through three innings without allowing a hit, while throwing 48 pitches. Woodruff had done his job, and Counsell's job would be to work through the remaining six innings with his bullpen. He nearly did it, too, with the first three relievers after Woodruff combining to shut out the Rockies on just one hit.

The Rockies tied the game in the ninth inning, but that could hardly be blamed on the strategy of pulling Woodruff after three. That strategy worked (and the Brewers won the game, anyway, in the 10th inning).

The Brewers chose traditional starters for the next two games. Even then, they didn't allow Jhoulys Chacin or Wade Miley to go deep—Chacin pitched five innings, Miley 4⅔—but neither one was an opener. The Brewers won both of those games, too, earning a four-day break before they would begin the National League Championship Series against the Los Angeles Dodgers.

For most teams, those four days would provide a chance to reset the starting rotation. The Brewers were again ready to try something different.

So while the Dodgers began Game 1 with Clayton Kershaw, one of the best starting pitchers in the game, the Brewers sent Gio Gonzalez to the mound in the first inning. Gonzalez is a two-time All-Star and had a 2.13 ERA in five late-season starts after the Brewers acquired him from the Washington Nationals, but he wasn't there to match outs with Kershaw.

Gonzalez was there to pitch the first two innings. He was there to get the Brewers to their strong bullpen. He was there because as a left-hander who would be followed by right-handed relievers, he forced Dodgers manager Dave Roberts into early decisions in his platoon-heavy lineup.

Gonzalez gave up a second-inning home run to Manny Machado, but that would be the only run the Dodgers would get until the eighth inning. He was the opener, and the strategy worked. The Brewers won the game, 6–5.

"It's exciting to see the revolution," Gonzalez told reporters. "I guess that's what it is."

If that is what it is, it spread rapidly in the latter part of the 2018 season. The Oakland A's, who were hit hard by injuries but more or less stuck to a traditional rotation through the first five months of the season, used reliever Liam Hendriks as an opener eight times in September. Hendriks pitched a scoreless first inning in each of the games, but the A's went on to win just four of them.

"Mixed results," manager Bob Melvin said. "Some games were good, some not."

Even so, when the A's made the playoffs as the American League's second wild-card team, they decided to use Hendriks as an opener in the Wild Card Game against the New York Yankees. The results weren't good. Hendriks allowed a two-run home run to Aaron Judge in the first inning, and the A's never recovered.

There's no way to know if they would have done better using a traditional starter. Their best starter during the season was left-hander Sean Manaea, but he had shoulder surgery in early September. They could have used Edwin Jackson, a veteran starter who had a 3.33 ERA in 17 games, but in a winner-take-all game where they could use a 10-man bullpen it hardly seemed ridiculous to piece it together and give the Yankee hitters different looks all night.

It just didn't work out.

The opener strategy is easier to use with a Wild Card Game roster, which is only set for one game and thus can be stacked with relievers. It's also easier to use in September, because the expanded 40-man roster means plenty of relievers are available. It's a bigger challenge from April through August. The Rays had the most bullpen innings of any team in baseball history in 2018, and there were times during the season it was a challenge for Cash to find fresh relievers.

There's no question teams will continue to experiment with using an opener in future seasons. There's also no question the use of traditional starters isn't going away anytime soon, because at this point every team would choose a true dominating starter to begin a game over using an opener.

The Houston Astros believe in analytics as much as any team, but they also believed in perhaps the strongest five-man rotation in the game in 2018, with Justin Verlander, Gerrit Cole, Dallas Keuchel, Charlie Morton, and Lance McCullers Jr. The Astros did start a few games with relievers, but those were more traditional "bullpen games" that teams have used for years, rather than an opener as part of a bigger strategy.

37

The Wade Miley Game
(or When a Probable Starter
Only Faces One Batter)

ONE ADVANTAGE OF USING AN OPENER IS YOU CAN FORCE
the opposing manager into uncomfortable platoon decisions.

Think about Game 1 of the 2018 NLCS, the one the Brewers
opened with left-hander Gio Gonzalez but only planned to use
him for the first time through the order. The Dodgers, who often
started David Freese at first base against left-handers but preferred Max Muncy against right-handers, put Freese in their
lineup that night against Gonzalez.

Freese flied out against Gonzalez to end the first inning. By
the time his spot in the order came up again, Gonzalez was out of
the game—by plan—replaced by right-hander Brandon Woodruff.
Even though it was just the fourth inning and no one was on
base, Dodgers manager Dave Roberts chose to pinch-hit Muncy,
giving him the platoon advantage against Woodruff.

But two innings later, when the same spot in the order came
up with two out and a runner on base, Woodruff had already
been replaced by Josh Hader, the best left-handed reliever in

the Brewers bullpen. At that point, Roberts had little choice but to stick with Muncy, who struck out.

Freese, one of the Dodgers' best right-handed hitters and one of their most successful hitters in the postseason, was already out of the game.

A similar situation developed in Game 5, when Freese again had just one plate appearance. But this time, the cause was as much deception as it was strategy. Or maybe we can just call it strategic deception.

One day earlier, the Brewers announced to the Dodgers and to the world that left-hander Wade Miley would be their Game 5 starting pitcher. Miley would be on short rest, but the way the Brewers were handling their pitching, that didn't seem so unusual.

What was unusual was what the Brewers actually had planned. While they told the world (and the Dodgers) Miley would be starting, what they didn't say was that he would only face one batter before being replaced by Woodruff, a right-hander. Miley would actually be their starter for Game 6 (which he did eventually start).

The plan was to bait Roberts into putting his right-handed hitters into the lineup. Woodruff would wait to begin warming up until the lineup cards had been exchanged before the game, locking those decisions into place. A right-handed batter listed on the official lineup could be pinch-hit for at any time, but he would then be out of the game and not available to use as a pinch-hitter later.

The Dodgers, perhaps sensing something might be up or that Miley wouldn't work deep into the game, started a different lineup than in Miley's first NLCS start, using two of their left-handed platoon players. One of those was Cody Bellinger, who led off and was the only batter Miley faced (he walked). Still, Woodruff faced a more favorable lineup than he likely would have had he been the announced starter. He pitched 5⅓ innings and allowed three runs. While he was out-pitched by Dodgers starter Clayton Kershaw and the Brewers lost the game, the strategic deception may have given them the best chance to win.

It definitely wasn't against the rules. Baseball has no rules about announcing probable pitchers, even though the practice goes back more than 100 years. (Researchers at the Hall of Fame found a reference to probable starters in a 1901 newspaper story!) And there's certainly no rule against removing your starter one batter into a game.

Remember, the Brewers had done just that in a September game against the St. Louis Cardinals. The only difference that night was that they started a left-handed reliever, and it was fairly obvious right away that he was only there to face Matt Carpenter, the Cardinals' lefty-hitting leadoff man.

In the case of Miley and Woodruff, it was the deception part of it that bothered some people, rather than the strategy part. But not everyone.

"If we swapped pitching staffs, we would probably be doing something similar to what they're doing and they would be doing something similar to what we're doing," Dodgers general manager Farhan Zaidi told the *Los Angeles Times*, comparing the way the two NLCS teams handled pitching plans in the series.

Had the Brewers won the game and/or won the series, perhaps more people would have complained. Perhaps baseball would have even instituted some rule requiring a starting pitcher to face a certain number of batters or record a certain number of outs, unless he leaves the game because of injury.

Perhaps teams will just stop listing probable starters, although that seems unlikely. While listing probables has been seen mostly as a courtesy to opponents, it can also help spur ticket sales for games involving aces. It also matters greatly to gamblers and to those playing daily fantasy games, some of which are now in commercial partnerships with MLB and individual teams.

Teams will continue to try for favorable batter-pitcher match-ups, which in essence is what the Brewers were attempting to do. But the strategic deception probably only works in a play-off series, and only with the right combination of pitchers and opponents. It's not like the Dodgers were going to have Kershaw face the opening batter of a game a day or two before he is really scheduled to start.

The Dodgers wouldn't do that with Kershaw. The Brewers wouldn't have done it if they had a Kershaw.

"Pick the five best starters in baseball," Brewers GM David Stearns told the *Los Angeles Times*. "[Jacob] deGrom, [Justin] Verlander, [Max] Scherzer—if we had those three guys at the top of our rotation, I think [Counsell] would be really comfortable. I don't think he'd have a problem letting those guys run out there."

And not to face just one batter.

38

You Can Start,
But You Can't Finish

LONG BEFORE THE OPENER CAME TO BE, THE ROLE OF A starting pitcher had already changed. Where once a starter went to the mound hoping to be able go the distance and win a game, in recent years starters have been taught to get the team to the later innings with a chance to win and then hand it over to the bullpen.

Zack Greinke of the Arizona Diamondbacks had a 1.66 ERA for the Los Angeles Dodgers in 2015. Jacob deGrom of the New York Mets had a 1.70 ERA in 2018. Greinke and deGrom each made 32 starts; each completed just one of those starts.

Jack Morris, who went into the Hall of Fame in 2018, never had fewer than four complete games in any season where he started at least 25 games. He ended his career with 175 complete games.

At the end of the 2018 season, no active pitcher had more than 38. No pitcher under 30 had more than 15.

That's 15 for a career. Morris completed 20 games in 1983 alone—and he didn't even lead the league (Ron Guidry had 21).

Warren Spahn had twice as many complete games as Morris (375). Spahn had 12 seasons with at least 20 complete games. Fergie Jenkins and Robin Roberts each had eight.

In their day, top starting pitchers never thought about coming out of games. It was their job to pitch nine innings, or even more if the game went extra innings. Jim Kaat tells the story of a 1964 game he pitched for the Minnesota Twins in Boston.

Kaat had a 12–2 lead when he gave up three runs in the seventh inning. At some point, Twins manager Sam Mele was going to take him out of the game.

"I told him to give the guys in the bullpen a rest," Kaat said.

He gave up three more runs in the ninth, but the bullpen did get a rest—and Kaat got a 15–9, complete-game win. That was in July. A month later, Bob Sadowski gave up nine runs in a complete-game win for the Milwaukee Braves. In the 54 years since, only one pitcher has given up as many as nine runs in a complete game he won—Burt Hooton in 1974 with the Chicago Cubs.

If Kaat wasn't coming out of a game when he allowed nine runs, he certainly wasn't coming out in the eighth or ninth inning when he had a chance at a shutout. It did happen, but just nine times in his 625 career starts. Compare that to the 180 times he had a shutout going and went all nine.

The game changed for starting pitchers, and the changes began long before analytics took hold in front offices. It's been more than 30 years—since Fernando Valenzuela in 1986—that pitcher had 20 complete games in a season. Only one pitcher this century has gotten even halfway to 20 in a season—James Shields of the 2011 Rays had 11. In 2017, no one even went eight innings 10 times.

The game has changed, and it's unlikely to change back anytime soon. Forget a complete game, which even if no one reaches base requires a pitcher to go through the entire batting order three times. In modern baseball, you have to be a special pitcher having a good game to even get the chance to face the opponent's best hitters a third time.

And even most aces don't get a chance to go a fourth time through.

In the entire 2017 postseason—that's 38 games, 76 starting pitchers—only two pitchers were allowed to face an opposing batter a fourth time in the same game. Justin Verlander did it for the Houston Astros in Game 2 of the ALCS. Jake Arrieta did it for the Chicago Cubs in Game 4 of the NLCS (and he only faced one batter a fourth time). Far more often, the starting pitcher was gone before the middle of the opposing order batted a third time, and sometimes well before that.

It was no different in October 2018, when there were 39 games and still just two pitchers who made it to the fourth time through the order (Verlander in Game 5 of the ALCS, Walker Buehler of the Dodgers in Game 3 of the NLCS). And even in those cases they were done after facing the leadoff hitter a fourth time.

It didn't matter whether the pitcher was cruising. It didn't matter if his pitch count was low. CC Sabathia had thrown just 77 pitches for the Yankees in Game 2 of the American League

Division Series against the Indians. He had retired 13 of the last 14 batters he faced.

But it was his third time through the order. Yankees manager Joe Girardi couldn't wait to get to the bullpen, to give those hitters a different look. Sabathia was out, in a game the Yankees led by five runs.

"That made no sense," Jimmy Rollins said on TBS a few days later.

It made sense to the guys who make decisions by the numbers, because the numbers say hitters have a better chance the more times they see the same pitcher in a game. In 2018, batters had a .784 OPS in their third plate appearance against a starting pitcher, compared to .700 the first time through and .720 in their first appearance against a reliever.

The numbers don't lie. But they also don't apply to every situation.

"Stop focusing on the computer," Gary Sheffield said on TBS, agreeing with Rollins. "Let your eyes tell you what you see."

It's more than just eyes. Managers can also look at a pitcher's history. They have numbers that show not only whether a pitcher is losing velocity but also whether his arm angle is changing (a sign of fatigue). The decision doesn't need to be one-size-fits-all.

Most often, though, it's close to that. The third-time-through rule has become as established as the 100-pitch rule. If a starter is nearing 100 pitches, it's time to think about a change. If the lineup is turning over and the leadoff hitter is coming to the plate for a third time, it's time to think about a change—if the manager hasn't made one already.

Look at what happened in Game 2 of the 2017 World Series. Dodgers starter Rich Hill had allowed just three hits in the first four innings. It was a 1–0 game. Hill's spot in the lineup wasn't coming up. But he'd already gone through the Astros' batting order two times. Despite the success, Dodgers manager Dave Roberts was concerned. Hill was out of there.

Removing his starter so early—and unnecessarily—meant Roberts ran through almost his entire bullpen by the ninth inning. It almost worked, but when closer Kenley Jansen gave up a game-tying home run in the ninth, Roberts had only Josh Fields, Tony Cingrani, and Brandon McCarthy remaining. It was hardly a surprise to see the Astros score two runs off Fields and two off McCarthy to win Game 2 and even up the Series.

When you're asking your bullpen to cover that many outs in one night, you're counting on way too many people to have a good night. Sometimes it's unavoidable because your starter didn't have it. But Roberts made the same move on a night his starter did have it.

Roberts took plenty of heat that night, but he was doing what he had done all postseason and really all season. He was doing, presumably, what the Dodgers' analytically inclined front office wanted him to do. Dodgers starters faced a batter a third time in the same game fewer times than starters on any other team in baseball in 2017. Four times in their first 10 postseason games, Roberts pulled his starter after he had gone through the order exactly two times (and in another game he pulled him one batter into the third time through). The only starter allowed to go deep in the game was Clayton Kershaw.

Until Game 2 of the World Series, the strategy worked. The Dodgers bullpen didn't allow a single run. The Dodgers swept the Diamondbacks in the Division Series and won the NLCS over the Cubs in five games.

"The way we've done things all year long, I know our players understand it, believe in it," Roberts said a day after Game 2. "I know I believe in it."

They were willing to run the risk of what happened in Game 2. It was an unnecessary risk.

Even in today's game, the smartest managers know to trust their eyes and the smartest teams let them do it. No team relies more on analytics than the Houston Astros, and general manager Jeff Luhnow knows all the numbers about the third time through the order. But in Game 2 of the 2017 ALCS, the Astros let ace Justin Verlander throw 124 pitches in nine innings. Verlander went the distance and faced 32 batters, meaning manager A.J. Hinch allowed him to face the middle of the Yankees order four times.

The last starter to face that many batters in an LCS game: Verlander, six years before in a win over the Texas Rangers.

"Those rules of thumb about times through the order, they're exactly that, rules of thumb," Luhnow said a couple days later. "There are some guys who have trouble the second time through. There are some that have trouble the first time through. In aggregate, I think the third time through is when most starting pitchers probably have trouble. It makes sense, logically, but when you have a pitcher like [Verlander] whose stuff seems to tick up later in the game, those rules don't apply."

He has to trust his manager, and the manager has to trust his eyes. Luhnow is willing to do that with Verlander, and more importantly with Hinch.

It used to be it was like that with every pitcher and every manager. Managers knew they had to watch some pitchers more carefully as the game went on, but they weren't nearly as quick with the hook. Just a decade ago, the 2005 White Sox had three starting pitchers with 25 more more games where they went through the order three full times. Twelve years later, in 2017, not one starting pitcher in all of baseball had 25 games like that.

Part of the reason is an increasing concern about pitch counts, to be sure. Part of the reason is that teams work harder on improving their bullpens. But a lot of it comes down to numbers. Most starting pitchers don't do as well the third time through the order. Chris Sale is one of the best pitchers in baseball, but batters went from a .282 slugging percentage the first time they saw him to a .408 slugging percentage if they saw him for a third time in the same game in 2017. Even as good as Kershaw is, opponents had a .297 slugging percentage the second time through, and a .438 slugging percentage the third time that same season.

It's so easy to talk yourself into bringing in a fresh arm, but there are plenty of times you're just doing your opponent a favor. Take Game 2 of the 2014 National League Division Series between the Giants and Nationals. Nats starter Jordan Zimmermann was one out from evening the series at a game apiece. The Giants had done absolutely nothing against him. He walks a guy with two out, and Nationals manager Matt Williams goes to his bullpen.

You don't have to guess what the Giants were thinking. They told us, after they tied the game off Drew Storen and won it in 18 innings.

"[Zimmermann] is one of the best pitchers in baseball," Giants pitcher Tim Hudson told Jayson Stark of ESPN.com. "So obviously, when you don't face him, you're not exactly pissed."

Not every starter is Zimmermann in October 2014. It's not ridiculous at all to pay more attention when your average starter gets deeper into a game.

In his 2016 book *Ahead of the Curve: Inside the Baseball Revolution*, MLB Network host Brian Kenny made the argument for what he called "bullpenning," redistributing innings in a way that hitters would almost never see the same pitcher three times. Kenny quoted 2014 MLB numbers showing hitters with a .755 OPS the third time they faced a starter, as opposed to a .682 OPS in their first plate appearance against a reliever.

But even Kenny says his ideal staff would include one "ace" who throws 220 innings (almost seven innings a game, if you assume 33 starts) and another starter who throws 200. Not a single team in the major leagues had two pitchers doing that in 2017. Only three teams had a pair of 200-inning pitchers. Not surprisingly, all three (the Red Sox, Nationals, and Indians) won their division.

In 2018, only one pitcher in all of baseball—Max Scherzer of the Nationals—threw 220 innings. Of the three teams with two or more pitchers who topped 200 innings, only the Arizona Diamondbacks missed the playoffs.

Kenny's premise is that you want to limit the innings thrown by your lesser starting pitchers. He advocates for using the opener, as the Tampa Bay Rays did in many games in 2018.

The trend in today's game has been to limit innings and exposure for almost every starting pitcher. That means more innings for the bullpen to soak up, and that means carrying more pitchers. Teams now routinely have more pitchers than position players on their 25-man roster.

One problem with that and with limiting innings thrown by your starters: it means more innings thrown by pitchers who wouldn't otherwise be in the major leagues. It also means if you do ask your starter to go deeper, he may not even know how to do it.

When starters routinely worked deeper into games, they learned to go through the early innings without using all their pitches. When they faced a batter for the third time, he wasn't seeing the exact same sequence of pitches he saw the first and second times up. Now starters know they're probably gone from the game before that guy comes up a third time. Why save anything for an at-bat they'll never see?

It was never that way in the past. Morris, who pitched in the major leagues for 18 years before retiring after the 1994 season, said he went to the mound hoping he could throw only fastballs to the first nine batters in a game.

"If I could do that, then they still hadn't seen my slider, forkball, or changeup," he said. "I had something different to throw them later, with the game on the line."

It showed. In 1983, when Morris had those 20 complete games and threw a league-high 293⅔ innings, opposing hitters had a lower OPS when they faced him for a third time in a game (.684) than when they faced him the first time (.706). Morris wasn't giving manager Sparky Anderson a reason to routinely take him out of a game at that point.

In the best-known game of Morris' career, he went through the opponents' order four full times and faced two batters a fifth time. It was October 27, 1991, and it was Game 7 of the World Series. Morris told Minnesota Twins manager Tom Kelly he wasn't coming out of the game, and fortunately for the Twins, Kelly listened to him. Morris threw 10 shutout innings in one of the most iconic pitching performances ever, with the Twins winning 1–0 on Gene Larkin's single off Atlanta Braves reliever Alejandro Pena.

Morris threw 126 pitches that night at the Metrodome. Looking back, he said he could have gone even longer, if needed.

"I could have gone 15," he said. "It was the last game of the season. There was no need to hold anything back."

It's been more than 40 years since a major league pitcher threw 15 innings in a game. No one has ever done it in the postseason (Babe Ruth threw 14 for the Red Sox in the 1916 World Series).

Morris never threw more than 11 innings in a game, but he did throw those 175 complete games.

"The funnest part about pitching was walking off the field with my teammates," he said. "The game's over and I was involved in all of it, not just part of it."

Pitching in a different era, Verlander had just 24 career complete games through the 2018 season. But he also had 53 other games where he finished the eighth inning. Verlander's idol as a kid was Nolan Ryan, who completed 222 of his 773 career starts (including 26 of 39 with the 1973 Angels).

"Every time I take the mound I have the mentality of trying to go nine," Verlander said during the 2017 postseason.

Few pitchers today would say the same thing. As well as deGrom pitched in 2018, he seemed to have no problem at all when Mets manager Mickey Callaway pulled him after eight shutout innings in his final start of the season, even though he was working on a two-hit shutout of the National League East champion Atlanta Braves. DeGrom told reporters he was happy because his goal had been to get the 10 strikeouts he needed to reach 1,000 for his career, and he did it with the final out in the eighth inning.

Some old-school scouts watching the game cringed at hearing that, but it's not deGrom's fault. In today's game, when the third-time through is already considered the danger zone, complete games are just not a realistic goal.

39

Bullpen by Gabe

WITH STARTING PITCHERS LEAVING GAMES EARLIER, EVEN with the lead, bullpen management becomes a bigger issue than ever. For much of the past three decades, that meant finding a closer who would normally pitch just the ninth inning and then building a bridge from starter to closer by finding one or two set-up men who would normally pitch the seventh and eighth innings when you have a lead.

That's not the way things always have been done, but it is the way it's been done for 30 years or so. There are good reasons for it, but also good reasons to ask if it's still the best way.

"I think philosophically, we all need to challenge the shit out of our own beliefs," Philadelphia Phillies manager Gabe Kapler said during a 2018 season in which he had been doing just that. "What we think, we need to constantly be asking ourselves, is that true? We should always be open to changing our minds."

After going through April and the first weeks of May with Hector Neris in a fairly traditional role as the Phillies closer,

Kapler decided he needed to make a change. But rather than name another closer to replace Neris or even using some form of closer by committee, Kapler chose to use his relievers simply by where he felt they would fit best in a game.

Over the course of the season, nine different Phillies pitchers recorded at least one save, tying a franchise record. While rookie Seranthony Dominguez led the team with 16 saves, Kapler would often call on Dominguez in the seventh or eighth inning with the game on the line, and then go to another reliever in the ninth.

On the next-to-last weekend of the season, with the Phillies in must-win mode to stay in the National League East race, Kapler had Dominguez start the sixth inning in a tie game against the middle of the Atlanta Braves order (Dominguez pitched a 1-2-3 sixth, but the Phillies lost the game by allowing five runs in the seventh).

It was "Bullpen by Gabe," as Phillies beat writer Scott Lauber wrote in the *Philadelphia Inquirer*.

And as much as it may have warmed the hearts of those who have long championed changing the way bullpens are run, Kapler operated this way with a significant caveat.

As he told Lauber midway through the season, "I can assure you if we had Kenley Jansen on our roster, he'd pitch the ninth inning."

In other words, Kapler does believe in a traditional closer role, but only if he has a traditional top-flight closer. He does believe pitching the ninth inning is different from pitching other innings, even though he also believes "the most important spot in the game creates very similar emotions to the ninth inning."

It's those emotions that make the difference, because obviously the actual pitching doesn't change. And just as obviously, the opponent's toughest hitters can come up in the seventh or eighth inning just as easily as they could in the ninth.

The difference in the ninth is there's no safety net. If a pitcher can't hold a lead in the seventh or eighth inning, his team could still rally to win. If the closer doesn't do the job in the ninth, the team usually loses and the clubhouse is silent.

Nothing makes a team feel worse than a ninth-inning loss. Nothing is more likely to generate quotes about how "That's one we should have won."

If the starting pitcher has a bad day, no one says it was a game you should have won. If the cleanup hitter goes 0-for-4, no one says it.

When the closer fails, everyone says it, and not every pitcher is built to handle that feeling.

"There's some development to pitching the ninth inning," Kapler said. "Sometimes the plug is pulled too early."

He's probably right on that, but most managers aren't willing to suffer through many ninth-inning losses before pulling that plug. The alternative, all too often, is to risk seeing the team's season go past the point of recovery.

It's why proven top closers still get paid much more than other relievers. Jansen, who Kapler referenced, got a five-year, $80 million contract from the Los Angeles Dodgers when he became a free agent after the 2016 season.

The money matters, and it's one reason using a bullpen with no set roles is so hard to do. Since relievers know they'll get paid based on saves and their ability to pitch the ninth inning, few top closers will react well if they're told a manager prefers to use them in high-leverage spots in the seventh or eighth.

The problem for baseball is that with starters pitching fewer innings than ever, managers much more frequently need relievers to protects leads in the seventh or even in the sixth. More creativity is required, and more managers are tempted to tell pitchers, "You want to know your role? Your role is to get outs when I tell you to pitch."

As good as that sounds, many pitchers perform better when they can predict when they'll be used and can mentally and physically prepare for it. And if managers have more or less established roles, it's easier for them to distribute work to their relievers in a way that avoids overuse and burnout.

It also limits how much a manager gets questioned about his bullpen use, because even in losses, fans, media, players, and front-office people are more forgiving when a manager simply follows a set formula. Varying from that formula may slightly improve the chances of success in any one game, but it also creates more confusion and more chances for second-guessing.

So what about bullpenning, the concept Brian Kenny has championed both on MLB Network and in his book, *Ahead of the Curve: Inside the Baseball Revolution*? Kenny believes a manager should use his best relief pitcher as a "relief ace" rather than as a traditional closer.

Kenny and others loved how Terry Francona used Andrew Miller during the 2016 postseason. Miller appeared in 10 of the Indians' 15 games, and each time he was asked to get more than three outs. Three times, Francona called on him as early as the fifth inning. Miller went through his first 16 innings without allowing a run and the Indians got to Game 7 of the World Series before losing to the Cubs.

It was brilliant pitching and brilliant managing, as Francona took advantage of both his available talent and the postseason schedule. With only a month to win a championship and off days liberally sprinkled in, he could use Miller, a true "relief ace," as Kenny would call him, in the key situation in every game.

Two key points: First, when the Indians acquired Miller and Francona began using him earlier in games, he said the only reason he could do it was his trust in Cody Allen as the Indians' closer. Francona is a thinking-man's manager, but he has an old-school sensibility in believing he still needs a closer accustomed to handling the final three outs of a game. Allen also appeared 10 times in that 2016 postseason, and in eight of those 10 games he was on the mound at the end.

The second key point is that while Francona was super-aggressive using Miller early in October games, he knew better than to try the same thing from April through September. Miller appeared in 57 games for the Indians in 2017, never as early as the fifth inning and just seven times before the seventh.

For the most part, Francona used Miller in a fairly traditional setup role in the regular season, having him enter a game in the seventh or eighth inning with a closer, Allen, behind him.

Why wouldn't you try to win regular season games just as much as you try to win in October? You have to make the playoffs before you can win them, right?

Of course you do, but if you start using a pitcher like Miller as soon as you think the game is on the line in the fifth or sixth inning, you're going to find yourself warming him up every night. Even if you don't bring him into every game, all those pitches thrown in the bullpen add up. Managers who use their bullpen too aggressively in April end up with relievers who are burned out by July.

Managers probably do pay too much attention to the dictates of the save rule, holding closers back for a save situation (a lead of no more than three runs, or the tying run on base, at bat or on deck for a pitcher entering mid-inning). But as long as pitchers get paid in part because of how many saves they get, it's hard for a manager to move away from that strategy.

There are top relievers who will tell you they'll pitch whenever the manager needs them. Miller is like that, but he was a 32-year-old veteran with a long-term contract. David Robertson said the same when he was traded back to the Yankees in 2017, but again he was a 32-year-old veteran with a multi-year deal.

And most managers don't have the luxury of having two or more relievers with that kind of experience. The Indians had Miller and Allen. The 2017 Yankees had Robertson and closer Aroldis Chapman, as well as other top relief arms in Dellin Betances and Chad Green. Plenty of other teams are trying to get by with a closer, perhaps a setup man or two and then a bunch of guys they wouldn't really trust to close out a game.

Is the ninth inning really that much different? Pitchers who get moved to the ninth always say they want to treat it the same. But plenty of those same pitchers find out the ninth is different, because of the adrenaline that shows up with the game on the line and because if they fail, the team usually is going to lose.

"It's coming down to you," said Shawn Kelley, who has pitched both as a closer and as a middle reliever. "You're high-fiving and you did your job or you're answering to the media on why you blew the game. You can screw up earlier in the game and your team still has a chance to win. [As a closer], you either do the job or you're the goat."

It's why teams are willing to pay big money to pitchers who have proven they can close. It's also why the unwritten rule that still holds says you don't use that closer until the latter part of the game.

40

Bullpen by Gabe, Part II
(or Position Players
Can Pitch, Too)

SPARKY ANDERSON MANAGED 4,030 GAMES IN THE MAJOR
leagues. Only six men in history have ever managed more.
He won five pennants and three World Series, two with the
Cincinnati Reds and one with the Detroit Tigers.

One more thing: Anderson never once put a position player
on the mound to pitch.

It didn't matter if the game went 19 innings, as one Reds
game did in 1972 (Anderson got through it with just three pitchers). It didn't matter if his team gave up 19 runs in the first
game of a doubleheader, as the Reds did one day in 1978 (he
used four pitchers in that game, and just two in winning the
nightcap).

It didn't matter. He considered it disrespectful to the game if
he put a non-pitcher on the mound, and he wasn't going to do it.

Gabe Kapler did it in the third game he ever managed.

Down 13–2 to the Atlanta Braves just two days after Opening
Day in 2018, with his starter having given him just eight outs

and four other actual relief pitchers already used and his bull-pen already taxed from overuse in the first two games, Kapler sent utility man Pedro Florimon out to pitch the eighth inning. Florimon gave up two runs, but at that point it hardly mattered.

What mattered to Kapler was he was saving some wear and tear on pitchers he might need the next day or the next week.

Kapler's bullpen strategies drew some criticism, especially early in the 2018 season, but he wasn't being disrespectful by putting Florimon on the mound. In today's game, with the emphasis on pitch counts and overuse of pitchers, he was simply being prudent. Teams all over baseball use position players to pitch now, more than ever.

At least Kapler planned for it.

"The only thing that has stopped us from using position players more frequently in blowout games in the past is fear of embarrassment," Kapler told Jared Diamond for a story in the *Wall Street Journal*. "Somebody has to be the one that says, 'I don't care that this looks embarrassing.'"

Kapler didn't want it to look too embarrassing, so in spring training he told his team he would sometimes use position players to pitch. He had Triple-A pitching coach Dave Lundquist work with Florimon and some other players who were most likely to be called on to pitch.

Some managers still don't believe in it. Mike Scioscia didn't do it in his first 18 years managing the Angels, until he used catcher Francisco Arcia in two blowout games in 2018. Dave Roberts of the Los Angeles Dodgers is another who doesn't like it, although he sent utility man Kike Hernandez out to pitch the 16th inning of a July 2018 game in Philadelphia. The Dodgers had already used eight actual pitchers in the game, and Roberts pinch hit for the eighth one while trying to score a run in the top of the 16th (they didn't, and Hernandez walked two and gave up a three-run walkoff home run).

In 2018, 25 of the 30 clubs used at least one position player to pitch. Kapler used four (including Florimon twice). Joe Maddon of the Cubs used five, including Anthony Rizzo, his All-Star first baseman.

Using a key position player on the mound has almost always been a no-no for a manager, at least since Kevin Kennedy put Jose Canseco on the mound for the Texas Rangers in 1993. Canseco was the everyday No. 3 hitter for a Rangers team hoping to contend, but he had been begging for a chance to pitch and Kennedy gave it to him when the Rangers were trailing 12–1 at Fenway Park.

The only problem? A few days after his 33-pitch stint—or stunt—Canseco complained of pain in his right elbow. Tests eventually showed torn ligaments, and by the All-Star break Canseco was having season-ending surgery.

Kennedy was ridiculed for losing a key player by putting him on the mound in a blowout, but the truth is that better players than Canseco had been used as pitchers before. Hall of Famer Jimmie Foxx pitched a scoreless inning for the Red Sox in 1939, in a year where he finished second in MVP voting. Ted Williams pitched two innings for the Sox in 1940, at his own request, with the *Boston Globe* story the following day reading, "Tempestuous

Teddy Williams, the Red Sox problem child, pitched at Fenway Park yesterday."

And in 1952, in the middle of his Hall of Fame career, Stan Musial threw one pitch for the Cardinals, in a gimmick arranged by manager Eddie Stanky.

Musial was on his way to a third straight National League batting crown, and Stanky decided it would be a great idea for him to pitch to Cubs outfielder Frank Baumholtz, who was just behind him in the batting race, on the final day of the season. Stanky brought Musial in to face Baumholtz, who hit a ground ball to third base and reached on an error. Musial returned to center field, never to pitch again.

"I didn't really want to do it," Musial told the *St. Louis Post-Dispatch* years later. "They wanted to bring some people into the park, knowing I was going to pitch to one hitter. I was leading Frank by five or six points in the batting race. If it had been any closer than that, I wouldn't have done it."

Even so, by the time Bob Brenly put Mark Grace on the mound for one inning when the Arizona Diamondbacks were being blown out by the Los Angeles Dodgers in September 2002, Brenly felt the need to explain himself to fans and to Dodgers manager Jim Tracy.

"I didn't intend to make a mockery of it," Brenly told reporters, adding that he was going to call Tracy and explain he wanted to save his other relievers.

Grace, who was 38 years old and near the end of a fine career, made the most of the chance to pitch, and also of the opportunity to take some of the edge off what was, at the time, the worst loss in Diamondbacks franchise history. At one point, he launched into an imitation of hefty D-Backs reliever Mike Fetters.

"My butt aches, my legs ache, my arm hurts," Grace told reporters. "But if you can have five minutes of fun in a game like this, then it's worth it."

Maddon and Rizzo obviously thought the same thing in 2018. Well, Rizzo certainly did. Maddon must have been holding his breath as one of his key players threw the two pitches it took him to retire A.J. Pollock on a fly ball and end the top of the ninth inning in a 7–1 Cubs loss.

"I promised Joe I wouldn't blow out [my left arm]," Rizzo told reporters. "You have to have fun with it and try not to embarrass yourself at the same time."

Rizzo said Maddon told him not to throw at maximum effort.

"He got his shot," Maddon said. "I don't want to hear it again, and he conceded he'll never pitch again."

So yes, in today's game you can use a position player on the mound without anyone accusing you of disrespecting the game. Every once in a while, you can even do it with one of your stars.

41

If a Big Game Is Tied, Shouldn't Your Best Pitcher Pitch?

CLOSERS WHO DO THEIR JOB WELL MAKE MANAGERS' JOBS easier. For years with the Yankees, Joe Torre (and then Joe Girardi) never had to worry about how to get through the ninth inning. Mariano Rivera took care of it. Torre could even go to Rivera in the eighth inning, which he did regularly in October as the Yankees were winning championship after championship. Rivera had 31 career postseason saves of four outs or more. No other closer has more than seven.

You get a lead. You hand him the ball. You shake hands after you win.

Simple.

But what happens if you get to the ninth inning and the game is tied?

Now it gets more complicated.

We'll start with the traditional unwritten rules governing closers: You always use him in a save situation in the ninth (leading by no more than three runs to begin the inning, tying run on deck with the inning in progress), unless he has worked too many days in a row. Every manager has a different guideline on how many days in a row are too many, and it can vary dependent on how much of a rubber arm your closer has.

You also use your rested closer in the ninth inning of a tie game at home, because at that point you're not going to have a save situation in that game. If you take a lead after that, the game ends. You don't have any more outs to get.

The tougher call is what you do in a tie game on the road, and it's a call bound to start arguments between old-school managers and new-school numbers guys. The traditional rule says you don't use your closer, because you could still have a save situation in extra innings. The numbers guys say by using a lesser reliever, you're running too big a risk of losing a game without your best reliever ever appearing in the game.

It's the Buck Showalter question, or the Zach Britton question, if you prefer. Showalter was the Orioles manager in 2016 and Britton was his standout closer. And in the American League Wild Card Game, which the Orioles lost to the Blue Jays in 11 innings, Britton never pitched. Seems like a problem, even if Showalter was following that traditional rule. The Orioles never led after the fifth inning, and they were playing on the road at Rogers Centre. Using Britton to keep the game tied risked needing to use someone else for a save if the Orioles ever took the lead. Showalter wouldn't do it, and when he brought in first Brian Duensing and then Ubaldo Jimenez to pitch the 11th inning, the Orioles lost the game and went home for the winter, wondering what might have been. The Blue Jays, on the strength of Edwin

Encarnacion's dramatic home run off Jimenez, moved on to the ALDS against the Rangers.

It's easy to say Showalter made the wrong decision, because we know what happened. The Jays moved on. The Orioles went home. Britton never pitched. But there were other reasons it turned out the way it did, besides not using Britton in a tie game. To start with, there was Showalter's choice to use Jimenez, who had pitched 21 innings against the Blue Jays during the season while giving up 15 runs. The only thing he had going for him was he was a starter and could give the Orioles multiple innings if he could keep the game tied. That wasn't much of a help when he couldn't make it through even one clean inning.

Joe Maddon faced the same questions—and the same criticism—after Game 2 of the 2017 National League Championship Series. Maddon left Cubs closer Wade Davis unused in the bullpen in the ninth inning of a 1–1 game at Dodger Stadium. Instead, he had Duensing (already in the game) begin the ninth inning, and then he went with John Lackey, a starter who was pitching on back-to-back days for the first time in his career. Perhaps predictably, Lackey walked Chris Taylor and served up a walkoff three-run home run to Justin Turner, giving the Dodgers a two games to none series lead.

How could you lose without using your best reliever?

"I really just needed [Davis] for the save tonight," Maddon responded.

Sorry, Joe. The save isn't important. The win—for the Cubs, rather than for any individual pitcher—is what matters, especially in a series you're already trailing. Pitching Davis in the ninth and extending the game gave the Cubs the best chance of winning, even if it meant being forced to use someone else (even Lackey) to close out the game after you score in the 10th.

Would they have scored in the 10th? No guarantees, obviously. Dodgers closer Kenley Jansen had thrown just 13 pitches in the ninth inning (pitching in a tie game at home). He likely could have gone at least one more. But the guy leading off the 10th for the Cubs would have been Addison Russell, whose fifth-inning home run gave the Cubs their only run of the game.

Maddon said he only had Davis for one inning, because three days earlier he had thrown 44 pitches in 2⅓ difficult innings to win Game 5 of the division series. But Maddon, for all his "new school" reputation, was actually very "old school" in how he used Davis, who was the Cubs closer for just one season before leaving as a free agent. Davis appeared in 59 regular-season games in 2017. Only one of those 59 appearances came in a tie game on the road.

The problem with using your closer when it's tied on the road is you still need to get at least six more outs to win the game. You need to get through the bottom of the ninth, score in the top of the 10th and get three more outs in the bottom of that inning. If your closer is mostly a one-inning pitcher, using him when it's tied means you're either committing to extend him beyond his comfort zone or to using a different pitcher if a save situation arises later.

The counter-argument is that you might score six or seven runs in the top of the 10th, and then anyone can close the game. And you don't even get a chance to play the 10th unless you get through the ninth, and often your closer gives you the best chance to do it.

The best option is to avoid a hard and fast rule. Instead, consider how much the closer has pitched recently, what part of the order is coming up in the bottom of the ninth, and, just as importantly, who would you have coming up in the 10th. After all, if you're not going to win the game in the 10th, someone else is almost certainly going to have to pitch, because it's very unlikely you'd ask the closer to get more than six outs.

In the 2016 Wild Card Game, Showalter had his middle of the order up in the ninth inning. Setup man Brad Brach had pitched the bottom of the eighth, and after the middle of the O's order didn't produce a go-ahead run, Showalter stuck with Brach to begin the ninth. He finished the ninth with Darren O'Day, another quality setup guy, and had O'Day pitch a 1-2-3 10th inning, as well.

At that point, Showalter had another decision to make. He had the Blue Jays' order about to flip over, with the ninth-place hitter leading off the inning but dangerous Josh Donaldson due up third and Encarnacion behind him. If he could get through the bottom of the 11th without losing the game, he had the middle of his order—Manny Machado, Mark Trumbo, and Matt Wieters— due up again in the top of the 12th. It was a perfect time to go to Britton, his best reliever. He went to Jimenez, and we know what happened.

No manager gets it right every time, not even one as good as Buck Showalter.

42

When You Play for One Run (or Is the Bunt Dead?)

EVEN THE WORST TEAM IN BASEBALL WINS MOST OF THE time after scoring the first run of a game. Even the best team in baseball loses most of the time when it doesn't.

Don't believe that? It's true. The 2017 Dodgers won 104 games, but they were 34–41 when the opponent scored first. The 2017 Giants finished 40 games behind the Dodgers in the standings, but the Giants were 42–38 when they scored first.

As good as the Boston Red Sox were in 2018, with 108 wins, they were 34–39 when allowing the first run of a game.

So why doesn't anyone ever play for one run again early in a game?

The simple answer is there are other numbers that show it doesn't make sense, with so many home runs hit and with the knowledge that bunts are usually a low-value play.

The first-inning bunt has almost completely disappeared in the major leagues. As recently as 1979, the Minnesota Twins sacrificed successfully 24 times in the first inning. By 2017, all

30 major-league teams combined had just 35 successful sacrifices in the first inning. Ten teams didn't have a single first-inning sacrifice all season; no team had more than four.

According to numbers from Baseball Prospectus, in 2017, teams score about 41 percent of the time when they began with a runner on first with no one out. Put that runner on second base with one out and the percentage goes down to 39. And that one out seriously lowers the chance at a big inning. Teams averaged .89 runs in an inning they began with a runner on first and nobody out, as opposed to .69 runs with a runner on second and one out.

Some bunts obviously result in hits or errors; some bunts don't move the runner over or worse yet, end up as a double play. Some speedy hitters will try to bunt for a hit, knowing that even if they're thrown out there's a good chance they get the runner into scoring position.

Those bunts for a hit are fine. But even for a team like the 2017 Cleveland Indians, who were 55–6 when they led a game after two innings, an early sacrifice bunt didn't make sense. Terry Francona's team rarely used them, with only 23 sacrifice bunts all season.

Compare that to the 1954 Indians, who had almost as many sacrifices (107) as they did wins (111).

No team bunts anywhere near that often now. American League teams, whose pitchers come to the plate only in inter-league road games, averaged just 18 sacrifices for the entire 2017 season. The only American League player who got to double-digits was Delino DeShields of the Texas Rangers, and many of his credited 13 sacrifice bunts were actually attempts to bunt for a hit.

DeShields' manager was Jeff Banister, who is more willing than most to call for a bunt. In one 2018 game in New York, Banister had outfielder Carlos Tocci bunt with runners at first and second in the fifth inning of a game the Rangers trailed 5–1.

Tocci was a 22-year-old who was batting .185 with no home runs at the time. He was batting ninth, and the bunt set things up for leadoff hitter Shin-Soo Choo, whose double drove in two runs to get the Rangers back in the game.

"The game of baseball never stopped being played by players based on their skillset," Banister said in explaining the bunt. "I'm an advocate of analytics, but they can't quantify the pressure a pitcher is under when you move the runners. I know the probabilities very well, but I know who's coming up, too."

The probabilities are based on all the players in a given season and all the situations. Managers are paid to know their players and their team. But most teams in 2018 believed giving up an out wasn't good strategy in almost all situations, unless they had a pitcher at the plate.

There was a time when the stolen base seemed to be going the way of the sacrifice bunt, but that's no longer the case. The stats say a steal can be worth the risk if the runner is successful at least 75 percent of the time. The best base stealers can top that 75 percent mark.

Dee Gordon was successful 79 percent of the time when he led the National League with 60 steals in 2017. Trea Turner was even better, with an 85 percent success rate on his 46 steals that season.

Alex Cora had the Boston Red Sox running more often after he took over as manager in 2018. It made sense, because the Sox had 125 steals while being caught just 31 times, for a team-wide 80 percent success rate.

"As long as that percentage is up there like the one we have, we'll keep running," Cora told reporters early in the season. "When it goes down—I think even 75 percent is giving outs away."

Francona's Indians ran even more often, with 135 steals in 2018, with a similar success rate to the Red Sox at 79 percent.

Overall, major-league teams averaged a steal every other game in 2018. As statistician, historian, and Red Sox executive Bill James pointed out, there were more stolen bases per game in 2018 than there had been in any season in the 1930s, '40s, '50s, or '60s.

As bad as it looks to make a lot of outs on the bases, the three teams that made the most outs on the bases in 2017—the Red Sox, Yankees, and Astros—were a combined 68 games over .500. Part of that is simply a result of having a lot of baserunners, but it also shows being aggressive on the bases isn't always a negative.

"You've got to think about the spot," Cora told reporters early in 2018. "Does it change our chances of scoring in that spot? Does it make a big difference? That's what I want them to understand."

If you don't ever make an out on the bases, it almost certainly means you're leaving runs or opportunities to score runs out there. You're not taking enough chances, and some of those times you played it cautious you would have scored an extra run.

Think about one of the most famous games in Red Sox history, and one of the most famous plays. It was Game 4 of the 2004 American League Championship Series and Francona's Sox were three outs from getting swept by the Yankees. They needed to score at least one run in that inning or their season was over.

Mariano Rivera walked Kevin Millar to begin the ninth, and Francona made the decision to pinch-run Dave Roberts—and the decision to have Roberts steal second base.

"I kind of winked at him as he was going up the steps [of the dugout]," Francona told the *Boston Globe* years later. "I wanted him to know, 'Hey, you can do this.'"

There was a risk Roberts would get thrown out, but Francona knew getting him to second base with no one out would greatly increase the Red Sox's chances of scoring the one run they needed to extend their season. The chances of getting two more hits off Rivera weren't good; to that point in his postseason career, he had faced 387 batters and allowed just 10 of them to score.

The Red Sox could have bunted, but that would have given them just two shots to get a game-tying hit against a guy who held batters to a .177 average in his first 67 postseason games. Roberts' steal gave them three shots. According to Baseball-Reference.com, the steal raised the Red Sox's chance of winning the game from 37 percent to 47 percent.

As it turned out, they needed just one shot. Bill Mueller followed the Roberts steal with a game-tying single. A David Ortiz 12th-inning home run gave the Red Sox one win, and before they were done they'd get three more over the Yankees and four over the Cardinals to win their first World Series since 1918.

As for Roberts, he got his first job as a major-league manager 12 years later with the Dodgers. His first year was 2016, and his team stole only 45 bases all season. Only three teams in the major leagues ran less than the Dodgers did.

A big part of the reason was that the Dodgers didn't have any real basestealers in their lineup that year. But it was also true that Roberts and the Dodgers' analytics-based front office were philosophically opposed to giving away outs. The 2016 Dodgers put down only 30 successful sacrifice bunts, the fewest in the National League and the third-lowest total in NL history at the time.

The Dodgers went to the National League Championship Series that year. They went to the World Series the next year.

So who's to say they should have played for one run?

43

Thou Shall Not Sacrifice an Out

IT'S NOT JUST THAT TEAMS DON'T BUNT AS OFTEN AS THEY once did. By 2018, some teams hardly ever bunted at all.

Take the Toronto Blue Jays, who had just five sacrifice bunts.

It wasn't a misprint, and it wasn't a lack of execution, either. If anything, it was an overstatement, because two of the times they got credit for a sacrifice, the batter was really bunting for a hit. And according to information from Baseball-Reference.com and review of game tapes, there was only one time all season a Blue Jays batter had unsuccessfully attempted to sacrifice.

Did the Blue Jays even have a bunt sign?

"We do have a sign," manager John Gibbons said, pausing a moment before delivering his punch line. "Nobody knows it."

Gibbons was speaking with about two weeks to go in the season, at a point when the Blue Jays still had just four credited bunts all year. Across the field, the New York Yankees began the night with 10 sacrifice bunts for the season, but third-base coach Phil Nevin admitted that was an exaggeration, too. Most of those were plays where the batter was bunting for a hit but got credit for a sacrifice because a runner advanced while the batter was thrown out at first.

"We do [have a bunt sign]," Nevin said with a smile.

Once a big part of baseball, the sacrifice bunt has simply gone out of style. While the Blue Jays were the record-setter, they weren't really an outlier.

Before 2018, the record for fewest sacrifices in a season was eight, by the 2016 Boston Red Sox. Four of the 15 American League teams finished the 2018 season with fewer than eight.

And while the overall National League numbers are skewed because many pitchers can't hit and thus are still asked to bunt, six NL teams were in single digits for sacrifice bunts by position players. The Philadelphia Phillies had just six all season, and all but two of those were players bunting for a hit.

Phillies manager Gabe Kapler said even on the rare occasions he does ask players to bunt, he still prefers they try to bunt for a hit rather than simply give up an out.

Kapler strongly believes in challenging baseball orthodoxy, but his reluctance to give away an out simply to advance a runner (or two runners) by 90 feet puts him closer to the mainstream today. Not only do the numbers show that bunting is most often a low-value play, but with more and more hitters in a typical lineup capable of hitting the ball out of the park, it just doesn't make sense to regularly give away outs.

As Earl Weaver wrote in *Weaver on Strategy*, "There are only three [outs] an inning, and they should be treasured. It's such a basic fact that fans sometimes forget it, but an inning doesn't last 15 minutes or six batters or 20 pitches; it lasts three outs. Give one away and you're making everything harder for yourself."

Weaver is also credited with saying: "When you play for one run, that's usually all you get. I have nothing against the bunt in its place, but most of the time, that place is in the bottom of a long-forgotten closet."

What's funny is that even with that belief, Weaver once had his Baltimore Orioles team put down 85 sacrifice bunts in a season. No team in the majors will reach that total in today's game, and very few will get halfway there. Even in his final season with the Orioles, when the AL had adopted the designated hitter rule and Weaver had become more bunt-adverse, the O's had 33 sacrifice bunts in 1986. It was one of the lowest totals in the majors that season; in 2018, it would have tied for the most in the American League.

There are still exceptions, depending on the hitter and the pitcher but also on the game situation. If you're in the bottom of the ninth inning of a tie game, the average number of runs you would score doesn't matter, because you only need one to win. The numbers still give you a better chance to win with a runner on first and none out than with a runner on second and one out, but the advantage is slight enough that other factors— who's hitting and who's pitching—could swing it the other way.

There's even more reason to bunt with a runner on second base and none out in the bottom of the ninth (or extra innings) with the game tied. Using numbers compiled by Tom Tango, the win expectancy goes up slightly (from .807 to .830) if you move the runner over to third.

That makes sense, because with a runner on third in that situation, the opponent has to bring the infield and outfield in. You go from needing a hit to win a game to winning it almost any time the batter makes contact. As long as it's not a ground ball or line drive directly at an infielder, or a pop fly or very short fly ball, you're going to score the winning run.

That's why one of the few times Kapler asked his player to sacrifice, it was in the 12th inning, at home, with a runner on second and no one out. J.P. Crawford, the next batter, was 3-for-29 at the time. Crawford bunted successfully and after the Cincinnati Reds walked Cesar Hernandez, Scott Kingery followed with a walkoff sacrifice fly.

The bunt worked.

It does work sometimes, even now.

44

Welcome to Japan,
Where the Bunt Still Lives

FOR A VISITOR FROM NORTH AMERICA, A PROFESSIONAL
baseball game in Japan or Korea is a familiar yet foreign experience. There's the grilled eel at the concession stand, the carefully
coordinated cheers and songs coming from the *oendan* section
in the outfield...

And the sacrifice bunt after the leadoff hitter reaches base
in the first inning.

True sacrifice bunts have nearly disappeared in the major
leagues, thanks to analytics that show they're rarely a smart play.
But even as analytics have started to cross the Pacific Ocean and
move into the Asian versions of the game, no team has yet aban-
doned the strategy of giving up an out to move a runner over.

Jim Allen, who has chronicled Japanese baseball for more
than two decades and now writes about the game for Kyodo
News, studied the 2017 season and found that of the 183 times
the leadoff batter for the visiting team reached first base, the
next batter attempted a bunt 51 times.

In most of those cases, we're talking about a real sacrifice attempt, too, the kind where the batter is actually trying to give himself up to get the runner over. There are a handful of major league hitters who will bunt in the first inning, too, but it's always because they're trying to bunt for a hit. Sometimes, they're just taking advantage of a shift that leaves no one guarding the third-base line. They may get credit for a sacrifice if they do it with a runner on base, but it's never designed that way, not in the first inning and most often not later in the game, either.

The true sacrifice bunt is just not a high-value play. The numbers show even a team that puts down a successful sacrifice will score fewer runs on average in that inning than a team that doesn't. Allen's numbers show that's just as true in Japan, where those 51 teams that attempted a bunt with their second batter scored an average of .76 runs in those innings, while the 132 that didn't averaged .9 runs.

Like their American counterparts, Japanese teams are paying more and more attention to numbers like that. But tradition dies hard in Japanese baseball, and tradition there says scoring the first run of the game matters more than almost anything.

One Japanese baseball executive guesses that some players who know the numbers understand the first-inning bunts are rarely if ever good strategy.

"They're probably saying, 'Aw, bunt again? This ain't working,'" the executive said.

Japanese teams were bunting slightly less often in 2018, but even the teams with the fewest bunts had more than nearly every team in the major leagues (despite playing fewer games).

"The bunts are going to be there forever," Warren Cromartie, who played 10 seasons in the major leagues and seven in Japan, told the *Japan Times* in 2018.

That may be true, because Japanese managers have always been more reluctant to accept change than their American counterparts. Then again, as the Japanese executive said, most teams over there have added an analytics department in recent years. Just as in MLB, launch angles, spin rates and shifts have become part of the everyday conversation. Younger Japanese players are much more likely to study video of themselves and their opponents, where their predecessors may have tried to solve everything with more hours of practice.

"While many managers still look at the game like in the old days, the game played by younger guys is changing," the executive said.

It's unlikely to change completely, simply because the game as played in each country is influenced by the culture in that country. Julio Franco, the former major leaguer who played in both Japan and Korea and spent 2017 and 2018 as a hitting coach in the Korean league, learned one of the differences early on.

"Here, a friend told me that, when you got a man on first and third, and there's a grounder to the shortstop, they don't try to break up the double play," Franco told The Athletic in 2018. "In the United States, I break up the double play so the run scores. Here, it's more of a friendlier game. In the United States, it's a hard-nosed game—and you have to adjust to it. As soon as you adjust to it, you're fine. But if you don't get adjusted to it quickly, it plays a mad trick on your game."

"In Japan, it's the Japanese way. In Korea, it's the Korean way, and I understand that. Most guys have to get adjusted to it."

That's equally true for players moving in the other direction. Players have come from Asia in greater numbers—35 Japanese-born players and 12 Korean-born players had at least one game in the big leagues in the last 10 years—and they've had to learn the unwritten rules and quirks of the game as it is played here.

And while we may think some of those players would be more comfortable playing the way they did growing up in Japan, that isn't always true. When I asked Dodgers pitcher Kenta Maeda if he misses the atmosphere of a big game in Japan, he said it was actually the other way around.

"For Japanese people to come and see this, being here, it's pretty cool," Maeda said through an interpreter. "I like this kind of atmosphere. The fact that people actually clap when there's a good play or a pitcher has a good outing. In Japan, you do hear the orchestrated band, but you don't necessarily hear actual clapping."

As for those first-inning bunts, Maeda does miss seeing them—but only when he's on the mound and he wishes the opposing team would do it.

"I actually liked that as a pitcher, because it was an automatic out," he said. "Over here, the hitters don't necessarily do that, so I find it harder."

There are other differences between the game as played here and the one played there, but some of those are changing, too. Velocities are rising in Japan, just as here. Home run rates are, too.

What hasn't changed in Japan is that the idea of a pitcher intentionally throwing at a hitter as retaliation for a slight or a batter on his own team being hit is almost unknown.

"In Japan, I think that's very rare that they do that," Maeda said. "I'm sure there is a rare case where it happens. I heard in Japan, there used to be a lot of retaliation, back in the day. But now I think it's close to zero."

Then again, retaliation has become rarer in the American game in recent years. So maybe baseball in Japan and the major leagues is becoming more similar.

Or maybe not. Listen to those orchestrated cheers.

And watch for those first-inning bunts.

45

You Don't Have to Concede a Run (Even in the First Inning)

NO MATTER WHAT THE UNWRITTEN RULE, THE BEST managers have always believed in challenging orthodoxy when the old way didn't make sense.

Jim Leyland knew that tradition says most of the time you play the infield back and concede a run on a groundout when there's a runner on third and less than two out early in a game. He just didn't agree with it, not with one out, not unless his team already had a bigger lead.

Routinely, when he did it in the early innings, someone would say, "Leyland must think this is going to be a low-scoring game."

Not necessarily. He just didn't believe in conceding an easy run when he didn't have to.

"From watching games when I managed in the minor leagues, I saw way too many times that a manager played his infield back and a guy hit a ground ball right at the shortstop," Leyland said. "If he'd had the infield in, the runner either holds or you throw him out at the plate. And what [cutting off the run] does for your pitcher's confidence is unbelievable."

Playing the infield in also put bigger pressure on the batter, who knew he had to do more than just make contact to drive in the run. The batter should understand that infield in means a better chance at a hit, but hitters don't always react that way.

So why not always play the infield in? Simple. It does give the batter a better chance at a hit. If you play the infield in with nobody out, you're risking a big inning. It's too important to get that first out, unless it's already the middle to late innings and it's a run you can't afford to concede. While Leyland almost always played the infield in with one out, he would play his infield back in the early innings with none out and a runner at third.

Even in later innings, playing the infield in can be a risk with runners at second and third. Play the infield back, and a ground ball scores one run. If that same ground ball scoots past a drawn-in infielder, two runs score.

A manager has to read the game and react, based on his preparation.

Everything comes into play. Who's on the mound for you? What kind of pitcher is he? Who's on the mound for the opposition? Is he Cy Young or does he give up his share of runs? How is your team swinging the bat? A manager should go through his mental checklist. Some may play it more by feel and some may play it by the book.

"It's a feel," said Ron Gardenhire, a major league manager for 14 years. "With no one out in the early innings, I always played them back. With one out or later innings, it was a feel. If you were facing Roger Clemens, that was one thing. You had to think about their pitcher, and about your pitcher."

The way Leyland saw it, with one out he would rather take the chance of a run scoring on a ball through the drawn-in infield.

"You can still get a double play and get out of the inning," he said.

But he wasn't going to hand you a gimme run on an infield out.

"People would say, 'You played your infield in with one out and Mark McGwire up, how could you do that?'" Leyland said. "I said, 'Mark McGwire hits home runs. If he mis-hits it and it goes to an infielder, I don't want a run to score.'"

46

You Can Make the First Out at Third Base (If You Play for Joe Maddon)

IT'S EASIER TO SCORE FROM THIRD BASE THAN FROM second. That should be obvious.

You're 90 feet closer to home plate. You can score on a wild pitch or a passed ball, a balk, an infield hit, a squeeze bunt, or a sacrifice fly.

It's worth going from second to third. But not if you risk making the first or third out of the inning.

That's the unwritten rule, anyway, the one many of us learn as soon as we start playing the game. Don't make the first out of an inning at third base, because you're already in scoring position if you hold tight at second base. Don't make the third out of an inning at third base, because even if you get there you can't score on an out.

"The risk—100-fold—is greater than the reward," Minnesota Twins manager Paul Molitor, a Hall of Famer as a player, told reporters after an early-season game in 2016. "Being safe doesn't make it right for me."

Molitor was explaining why he had pulled outfielder Eddie Rosario from a game after Rosario stole third with two out. Rosario saw that Detroit Tigers third baseman Nick Castellanos was shifted well away from the bag. He took off for third and he was safe.

That wasn't good enough for Molitor or for the Twins front office, which sent Rosario to the minor leagues the next day. The reward of getting to third didn't match the risk of ending the inning, especially with the Twins down 5–0 in the seventh inning.

But as with so many of the unwritten rules, not everyone agrees that this one should still apply.

Joe Maddon wants his baserunners to have an aggressive mindset, and he'd rather risk the out than do anything that goes against that.

"I don't mind making the first or third out at third base," Maddon told author Tom Verducci in *The Cubs Way: The Zen of Building the Best Team in Baseball and Breaking the Curse.* "I don't give a rip—as opposed to using that line, which you've heard a hundred thousand times. I like to get to third base with less than two outs as often as possible. That's what we say.

"If everything is set up right and you're making your reads and this guy makes a great play, so what? I'd rather us be aggressive at third, even making the first out there. But to make the first out at *home* would really bum me out. I don't like that at all. It really fries your oysters."

There is a significant advantage to getting to third base, even with two out. Besides being able to score on a wild pitch, passed ball, balk, or infield hit, the threat of giving up a run on a pitch in the dirt can affect the way the pitcher feels comfortable attacking the batter at the plate.

But if you get thrown out at third, that batter doesn't get a chance at all, at least not with you standing in scoring position.

The unwritten rule about not making the first out at home—the one Maddon does subscribe to—came about for the same reason as the third-base rule. If you're on third base with nobody out, your team has two chances to get you home on an out. You even score on a double-play grounder. Best-case scenario, your team is set up for potentially a big inning.

Making the first out at home would cancel all of that out. It really isn't worth the risk.

As Verducci points out, Maddon is often willing to go against "The Book," to use another word for the unwritten rules. He once ordered an intentional walk that moved the tying run to third base and the winning run into scoring position at second, and it worked. He had Josh Hamilton walked with the bases loaded (and won that game).

Maddon told Verducci that he had to try different things when he was managing the small-market Rays against the giants of the American League East.

"If you try to go with the conventional, you are going to get your brains beat out," he said. "They have greater ability to win with more tried-and-true than you do."

Now that he's in Chicago managing the Cubs, Maddon has the team with that "greater ability to win." He doesn't need to be as unconventional—but he would still prefer aggressive baserunners, even if it means making the first or third out at third base.

Most others still hold to the rule, but players and base coaches break it all the time.

It happened to the Yankees in Game 2 of the 2017 ALCS. Brett Gardner hit a ball into the right-field corner with two out in the third inning of a scoreless game. Gardner had a chance at a triple and, in fact, he was initially called safe as he slid into third base. With the aid of video replay, though, he was called out. He was waved on to third base by an anxious third-base coach (Joe Espada), and he knew he was out before they even went to review.

It doesn't matter that it was a close play, or that it took a perfect relay throw from Carlos Correa to get him. With two out in the inning, it's a chance you just can't take. It felt worse because Aaron Judge was due up next, but it's a chance you don't take no matter who is at the plate.

There's no way to know if Gardner would have scored had he held at second. What we do know is the Yankees didn't score in the inning, and they went on to lose the game, 2–1.

It's surprising how many players still take that chance. In the 2017 season alone, 14 baserunners were thrown out trying to steal third with two out, many bringing a reaction from the manager similar to the one Royals manager Ned Yost had when Alcides Escobar was thrown out with Lorenzo Cain at the plate in the eighth inning of a 3–3 game.

"You've got to make sure you can steal the base," Yost told reporters. "There's gotta be no question. It's gotta be like 99 percent, you know. That didn't work out, pushing the envelope."

Yost would likely have had no problem had Escobar tried to steal third with one out.

By getting to third with one out, you can score on an out. You might even force the other team to play the infield in, improving the chances that the next batter gets a hit. You might even make the pitcher and catcher think twice about throwing a two-strike breaking ball in the dirt, because of the risk it goes to the screen and costs them a run.

So why doesn't the same apply with no one out? You can still score on an out, and you still score if the ball gets to the screen. The difference is you have two chances to get the run home from second base. You have a better chance at a big inning. It's not yet worth taking the risk on an out.

It's still not as bad as making the third out at third base.

47

You Can Pick Your Poison

SPARKY ANDERSON LOVED THE INTENTIONAL WALK. HE thought it was one of the greatest gifts the baseball rules gave to a manager. If they were going to let you choose not to face the best hitter in the other lineup, he was going to take advantage any time he could.

Year after year, Sparky would lead the league in issuing intentional walks. If he looked at the stat sheet and he wasn't leading, he'd actually look upset. In Anderson's mind, that meant he wasn't taking enough of the opportunities the game handed him.

But even Anderson never intentionally walked anyone with the bases loaded.

Buck Showalter did that, when he was managing the expansion Arizona Diamondbacks in 1998. The D-Backs went 65–97 that year, but one of the wins came on May 28 in San Francisco. With two out in the ninth inning that night, Showalter's team held an 8–6 lead with Barry Bonds coming to the plate.

Not only was Bonds maybe the most dangerous hitter in baseball, but he was also red-hot, with 15 hits in his last 36 at-bats (.417), including four doubles and three home runs. With two out and the bases loaded, even a single from Bonds would have given the Giants a win.

Showalter wasn't taking a chance, especially with closer Gregg Olson already having thrown nearly 50 pitches in the game.

"I was physically done," Olson remembered years later. "I'd come in the game in the eighth inning to face Bonds, and I still think I struck him out, but [home-plate umpire Ed Montague] wouldn't call the 3-2 pitch a strike. But Barry had seen my best stuff in the eighth, and that was when I was still strong. By the time he came up in the ninth, I was exhausted."

Showalter put up four fingers to call for the intentional walk. Catcher Kelly Stinnett looked at Showalter, looked around the bases to remind himself they were loaded, and then looked back.

Showalter had made up his mind. Bonds would be intentionally walked, forcing in the Giants' seventh run but taking away Bonds' chance to tie or win the game.

"It was the best opportunity to win the game," Showalter said.

Sure enough, it worked. After Olson intentionally walked Bonds, he got Brent Mayne to line out to right field to end the game.

At Candlestick Park, the visiting dugout was on the third-base side. The visiting clubhouse was down the right-field line, accessible by a door that led directly to the playing field. Olson went straight there after the final out, not even bothering to stop by the dugout to pick up his jacket.

"As I came in, [teammate] Willie Blair handed me a Bud Light and said, 'Damn, you're fun to watch.'" Olson said.

Olson sat down and tried to process what he'd just done. Eventually, reporters told him it was the first bases-loaded walk in a major-league game since 1944, when New York Giants player-manager Mel Ott ordered pitcher Andy Hansen to walk Bill Nicholson of the Chicago Cubs. Ott himself was the last batter before that intentionally walked with the bases loaded, in 1929.

When the reporters left, Olson went in to talk to Showalter.

"The next time we do something that hasn't been done in 54 years, can we have a mound conversation to talk about it first?" Olson asked. "I could have just hit [Bonds], and no one would have said anything about it."

In reality, Olson doesn't mind his small place in intentional-walk history. He's not even the last to issue one with the bases loaded. In August 2008, then–Tampa Bay manager Joe Maddon had pitcher Grant Balfour give one to Josh Hamilton, then with the Texas Rangers.

That one worked, too.

Still, it's been another decade since 2008, and no one else has tried it. But Showalter ordered another unconventional intentional walk late in the 2017 season.

It was the ninth inning. Showalter's Orioles led the Yankees 6–4 with two out and a runner on second base. Aaron Judge was coming to the plate.

Showalter ordered him intentionally walked.

He put the tying run on base. He brought the winning run to the plate. He chose to do it, violating the unwritten rule that says you never put the tying or winning run on base with an intentional walk.

Showalter had his reasons. Judge had killed the Orioles all season, with 11 home runs and 24 RBI in 19 games. The Orioles hadn't exactly handled Sanchez, either (he was hitting .368 against them with 12 RBI in 10 games), but he hadn't killed them as much as Judge had.

Anyway, Showalter broke the rule and got away with it. Britton struck out Sanchez, the game was over, and the Orioles had a win.

"They're both really good hitters," Showalter said. "You're really just picking your poison."

That's true, but one poison risks tying the game. The other risks immediately losing it.

Showalter's choice between facing Judge and facing Sanchez wasn't as clear as between facing Bonds and facing Mayne, but Anderson likely would have approved. Sparky always believed that the intentional walk gave a manager a choice of avoiding the other team's most dangerous hitter.

In his nine seasons managing the Cincinnati Reds, Sparky had Willie McCovey walked 22 times. He said years later he wished he had done it even more, no surprise given that McCovey still managed to hit 23 home runs and drive in 65 runs in 118 games against Sparky's Reds.

"Who do you think I am, Babe Ruth?" McCovey asked Anderson, in a story Sparky loved telling later in his career.

"No," Sparky replied. "You're better."

Once Anderson moved to the American League with the Detroit Tigers, George Brett became his favored target. Anderson had Brett intentionally walked 28 times in 15 seasons. He also walked Eddie Murray and Don Mattingly 20 times apiece, and Ken Griffey Jr. 19 times (in just seven seasons).

Anderson ordered his pitchers to avoid Griffey even when they weren't intentionally walking him. In one three-game series in May 1993 at Seattle's Kingdome, Griffey walked six times in 15 plate appearances. Finally, in the eighth inning of the final game of the series, Griffey came to the plate with runners at first and third and the Mariners just having taken a 6–5 lead.

It made no sense to walk him in that spot, and Anderson had Bill Krueger pitch to him. That went even worse, with Griffey hitting a long three-run home run. As he crossed the plate after rounding the bases, Griffey grabbed his crotch and stared at Anderson in the Tigers dugout.

As Larry Stone wrote 11 years later in the *Seattle Times*, Griffey and Anderson had history that went beyond a few intentional walks. Griffey's father played for Anderson with the Reds, and Anderson had Merv Rettenmund pinch hit for him with the winning run on base in the 10th inning of Game 3 of the 1975 World Series.

Later in that 1993 season, after the Tigers had thrown a few inside pitches to Griffey Jr., Ken Sr. told the *Seattle Times:* "Sparky wanted to get revenge. He has always been a vindictive [bleep]. I played for him for six years, so I know."

That may well have been true, but Anderson didn't keep walking Junior because of old feelings about his father. He walked him for the same reason he walked McCovey and Brett: They were the hitters he didn't want beating him.

Anderson would even use the intentional walk in the first inning. He did that twice with Brett and eight times with McCovey.

Just before Game 1 of the 1984 American League Championship Series, Anderson was talking to Mike Downey, then a columnist with the *Detroit Free Press*. He told Downey he'd even be willing to walk Brett with the bases loaded, although he never ended up doing that (at least not intentionally).

"That's the way they pitched Ted Williams," Downey told him.

"This guy may *be* Ted Williams," Anderson responded.

"I ain't sayin' don't never pitch to him," Anderson said, as recounted by Downey a decade later. "I'm sayin' don't let Brett beat ya. If my team's winnin' and it's late in the game and Brett's got a chance to beat me, I ain't pitchin' to the guy, no way. Bases loaded, shoot. I'll take my chances with whoever the hell's on deck."

The funniest part of all this: Brett didn't have a single walk in that ALCS. Not an intentional walk. Not an unintentional walk.

Then again, Brett also didn't beat Anderson in that series. The Tigers swept the Royals in three games and went on to beat the San Diego Padres in the World Series.

Mike Scioscia did walk Alex Rodriguez intentionally three times in the 2009 American League Championship Series. A-Rod wasn't always a big postseason threat, but that October he hit .455 with two home runs in the Division Series against the Minnesota Twins and .429 with three homers against Scioscia's Angels.

The first of those home runs came off Angels closer Brian Fuentes in the 11th inning of Game 2, tying a game the Yankees would go on to win in 13 innings. And it was that home run that set up an unusual strategy Scioscia would use twice in the next three games.

In Game 3 and again in Game 5, first in a tie game in the ninth and the second time with the Angels leading by a run in the final inning, Scioscia would have Fuentes walk A-Rod intentionally with nobody on base.

He was putting the winning run (in Game 3) and the tying run (in Game 5) on base. He was breaking an unwritten rule of the game.

Scioscia understood as well as anyone that what he was doing was unconventional. He was also completely convinced he was doing the right thing.

"In that situation you just want to keep Alex in the park," Scioscia said after Game 5.

In Game 3, it worked perfectly, with Fuentes retiring the next batter and the Angels going on to win in 11 innings. In Game 5, it nearly backfired. Fuentes followed the intentional walk with an unintentional walk and a hit batter to load the bases, before Nick Swisher popped up a full-count pitch to end the game.

The game would be remembered more for John Lackey yelling "This is mine!" when Scioscia came to the mound to take him out. The postseason would be remembered more for the Yankees winning their 27th World Series title.

But in that ninth inning, the story was Scioscia going against the unwritten rules and surviving for another day.

48

You Can Break Up a Double Play

ADAM EATON'S PAGE IN THE WASHINGTON NATIONALS 2018 media guide lists him at 5'9", 176 pounds. His stats page on Baseball-Reference.com will tell you Eaton has hit 41 home runs, not in one season but in all seven of his major-league seasons put together. While he's fast, he's not Billy Hamilton fast or Trea Turner fast. According to MLB.com's Statcast, Eaton's average sprint speed of 27.5 feet per second ranked 246th in the major leagues in 2018.

If Eaton is going to have value to justify the $8.4 million the Nationals are set to pay him in 2019, he has to generate it in other ways. He has to play the game hard while still playing it fair.

He has to do things like he did in the first inning of an August 1, 2018, game at Nationals Park. Eaton had led off the inning with a single, and when Turner followed with a ground ball to shortstop, Eaton understood his one and only job was to make sure the Mets couldn't turn a double play.

Ever since Mets shortstop Ruben Tejada suffered a broken leg on a Chase Utley slide in the 2015 playoffs, breaking up double plays has become trickier. What once was a staple of baseball's unwritten rules—the runner went in as hard as needed and it was the middle infielder's responsibility to get out of harm's way—became much more complicated when the so-called Utley rule went into effect before the 2016 season.

In the simplest terms, a runner now must begin his slide before reaching the base, must be able to reach the base with his hand (and attempt to do so) and not slide past it. He also can't change his path to move toward the fielder rather than the base.

It doesn't say you can't break up a double play, but many baserunners seem to have no idea how to use a slide that is legal under current rules. They either don't try, or they do what Manny Machado did in the 2018 National League Championship Series.

Machado, playing for the Los Angeles Dodgers against the Milwaukee Brewers, twice slid into second with his arm raised to interfere with infielder Orlando Arcia. The second time, when Machado actually grabbed Arcia's knee as he slid past, replay officials awarded the Brewers a double play.

Eaton made a point of learning what he could and couldn't do.

In that 2018 game against the Mets, Eaton went in hard but he went in consistent with the current rules. Mets second baseman Phillip Evans suffered a broken leg on the play, but only because he set up on the first base side of the bag as he took the throw from shortstop Amed Rosario.

The Mets challenged the play, insisting Eaton would have slid past the base if he hadn't run into Evans first. But the umpires on the field and in the replay center ruled Eaton's slide legal, and Major League Baseball issued a ruling agreeing with that call.

"Really the only contact left in the sport is at second base," Eaton said. "There's still contact. I think they've allowed middle infielders to kind of fall asleep at the base thinking guys are going to go off and not slide in. But realistically, we can still hit people as long as we touch the base and slide into the base. If you're in our way, then you can get hit.

"There's still contact, but middle infielders can get away from it. As long as they step and step far enough away from the bag, I can't touch you."

Eaton has learned to stay within the rules while still going in with the intent of making it harder to turn two.

"It gives me value," he said. "Some of the guys that aren't as fast can't get to the bag as quickly and can't break it up. It adds value to little players that can get a good jump and break up a double play. Maybe he throws it into the bench and now all of a sudden we've got a guy at second base. When you take that away, it devalues the guy who is kind of scrappy and grindy that wants to go out there and do the small things."

Eaton is right that because of the new rule, most baserunners don't even attempt to interfere with the second baseman or shortstop. Because of that, more and more middle infielders play as if the rule itself will protect them.

The best baserunning coaches, though, make sure their players know what they can and can't do. The best infield coaches make sure their players protect themselves as if every baserunner is still coming at them.

"To be honest, I haven't changed the way I coach it," said Perry Hill, widely acknowledged as one of the game's best at coaching infielders. "I like the throw to be at the back of the base. I want him to be able to catch the ball and let the base protect him."

If the infielder is at the back of the base, the runner would need to go through the base to take him out. That's much less likely to happen, and also much harder to do under the current rules.

Some players and coaches grumbled when the new rule went into effect, believing not only that it took away from the game but also that it was unnecessary. On the Utley play, they argued, Tejada only got hurt because he put himself in a poor position as he took the throw from Mets second baseman Daniel Murphy. Tejada took the throw as he was coming across the bag, with no real chance to double up Howie Kendrick at first. But rather than continue past the base, he did a spin so that his back was to Utley as the baserunner made contact.

Utley's slide was hard, and it may even have violated the previous rules for breaking up a double play. The umpires on the field let it go. MLB later handed Utley a two-game suspension, but dropped that before an appeal could even be heard.

"There wasn't anything clear-cut [in the old rules] to say that play violated a rule," MLB Chief Baseball Officer Joe Torre told the *Los Angeles Times*.

Since Utley went far beyond the base after making contact with Tejada, his slide clearly would have violated the new rule.

But even though that rule was intended to limit injuries and keep more of baseball's stars on the field, it still hasn't been fully accepted by everyone in the game.

"I'm not a big fan," said Hall of Fame shortstop Alan Trammell. "Being brought up in the era I was, we were taught to be aggressive but fair. And there's a way to do it."

Trammell cited Kirk Gibson, his former teammate and close friend, who was known for his willingness to take out a second baseman or run into a catcher to score a run.

"He was trying to get you, but he was trying to do it clean," Trammell said. "And that's how he was. You know what, middle infielders respect that. I don't want to get hit, but I'm going to try to get out of the way as well. Sometimes you've got to stand your ground."

As Trammell knew, there were ways for middle infielders to keep runners from bearing down on them too hard.

"We were taught, all the way back to when I was in youth baseball, to throw the ball right at their head," Trammell said. "They'll get down. Trust me."

Trammell retired long before the rule was changed, but his view is similar to the one veteran second baseman Dustin Pedroia expressed after a play he was involved in in May 2017. Manny Machado, then playing with the Baltimore Orioles, went in hard on Pedroia to break up a double play. Pedroia's Boston Red Sox manager John Farrell argued that Machado's slide violated the new rule (and a Red Sox pitcher later threw at Machado in a bit of retaliation that Pedroia quickly distanced himself from).

"I don't even know what the rule is," Pedroia told reporters at the time. "I've turned the best double play in the major leagues for 11 years. I don't need the [expletive] rule, let's be honest. The rule is irrelevant. The rule is for people with bad footwork, and that's it."

A colorful answer, but Pedroia basically said what Hill and other infield coaches have said, which is that infielders who made the play right could usually find a way to stay out of danger. And if they couldn't, so be it.

Former major-league manager Bobby Valentine agreed, saying he loved the athleticism required of middle infielders and calling the rule change "the biggest mistake baseball ever made."

Valentine had plenty of company the first year after the change, when uneven enforcement let to more confusion and more complaints.

"It's a joke," Toronto Blue Jays manager John Gibbons said, after umpires ruled a Jose Bautista slide illegal and gave the Tampa Bay Rays credit for a game-ending double play. "Maybe we'll come out and wear dresses tomorrow. Maybe that's what everybody's looking for."

Eventually the complaints became rarer, in part because it became rarer to see a runner try to go in hard at second base. All too often, runners give up on plays, not understanding that the new rules do give them somewhere to go.

You can still break up a double play. Just ask Adam Eaton.

49

You Can Argue a Call (but Many Don't)

NEXT TO THE BAT RACK AND THE SHELVES WHERE THE batting helmets are kept, there's a small card taped to the wall in the New York Mets dugout. It lists the umpires for that day's game, with the first names in large print.

Major-league umpires appreciate when players call them by their names. Some demand it.

"We're all professionals here," said one umpire, who makes sure he knows how the players want to be addressed on the field, too.

You wouldn't always know it, but the relationship between umpires and many players and managers often is a lot more cordial and collegial than adversarial. Arguments still happen, because it's an emotional game and careers can turn on wins and losses. But Major League Baseball introduced video replay to review home run calls in 2008, and went to a much more extensive replay review system in 2014. Players and managers can still complain about balls and strikes, which aren't subject to review, but it's much less common to see a manager on the field ranting and raving at an ump.

The Philadelphia Phillies, in fact, went the entire 2018 season without having a player, coach, or manager ejected from a game. By the end of 2018, no Phillies player has been ejected from a regular-season game since since June 16, 2015, according to Matt Gelb of The Athletic.

Ejections haven't disappeared—there were still 185 of them during the 2018 season, according to the UEFL Portal, which tracks them—but it's pretty safe to say no one will challenge Hall of Fame manager Bobby Cox's record. Cox, who managed 29 seasons in the big leagues, was thrown out of 158 games, plus three more in the postseason.

Bobby Valentine didn't come close, with 43 ejections in his 16 seasons as manager, but Valentine is among those who long for the days when you could go to a game and see a manager ranting and raving, perhaps throwing his cap or even a base, or mocking the umpire by covering the plate with dirt.

"It became something of a fun event," Valentine said in a 2018 interview on FanCred. "No one ever wound up in a fight. There was never anyone taken away in a police car. But it was really cool entertainment."

It's hard to argue with that, but even harder to argue with the idea that it's better to correct calls that were obviously wrong. Before replay was brought into the game, everyone could see within seconds that the umpire had blown a call. Everyone, that is, except for the umpires themselves, and they were the only ones who could change the call.

The use of replay brought along unintended consequences. The combination of high-def TV and ultra-slow motion proved that baserunners sometimes come off the bag slightly while sliding into a base, so infielders are now coached to hold a tag on a runner as long as possible. Debate continues over how long managers should be able to hold up a game while deciding whether to challenge a call, and how long the replay umpires can take before making their decision.

Ultimately, it would make the most sense for baseball to acknowledge that replay is useful when it eliminates the obvious wrong call. For the calls that are so close that they require multiple angles and stop-action, using replay slows the flow of the game and it would be best to let the original call stand.

Umpires, for the most part, welcomed the use of replay. They don't like getting calls wrong, and they especially didn't like watching highlight shows after a game that showed their mistakes over and over.

They didn't mind the arguments, and many of them had a good relationship with Cox, even after throwing him out of games. One of Cox's ex-players in Atlanta tells the story of one game where Cox was thrown out and spent the rest of the game in a room off the tunnel to the Braves clubhouse.

The umpire who had thrown Cox out of the game had to use the restroom between innings and walked into that tunnel. The player watched, wondering if the argument was about to start up again.

It didn't. Cox saw the umpire, asked if the crew had dinner plans that night, then made them a reservation at his favorite restaurant.

50

You Can Run (but You'd Better Know the Score)

WHEN HE WAS COACHING FIRST BASE WITH THE PHILLIES, Juan Samuel remembers a young player getting on base and noting the opposing pitcher had a high leg kick and would thus be easy to run on. "I think I can steal second," the player told him.

Samuel was happy the young guy was paying attention to the pitcher. He also realized the kid wasn't paying attention to the game at all. Either that, or he just didn't understand. The problem: the Phillies held a big lead at the time. It wasn't the time to go.

"You might not want to run right now," Sammy told the kid. "They might hit somebody."

Sammy knew plenty about stealing bases. His 72 steals in 1984 set a modern major-league record for the most by a rookie (although Vince Coleman topped it with 110 the following year). But Samuel also knew about when not to steal. He knew the unwritten rules of the game.

"I had the green light all the time," Samuel said. "If it was late in the game and I knew we needed baserunners, I'm not trying to steal a bag. I'm not taking a chance at getting thrown out. We need a big inning. If we're up by five runs late in the game, I'm not running."

It goes back to the larger unwritten rule that says you don't show anybody up. Some people will say if you guarantee you're not going to come back, or that you're not going to hit home runs when you have a big lead, I won't run when I have one. That's a reasonable point, but as Samuel told the kid at first base, if you run with a big lead, they might throw at someone.

Samuel took a similar approach when he was coaching third base. If his team had a big lead, he'll only send runners home if it's a no-brainer they'll be safe. There are actually two reasons for that. Beyond not showing anybody up, you don't want to run any risk of injury on a play at the plate in a lopsided game (although the rules on blocking the plate and not running into the catcher lessen that risk now).

But what's a big lead? At what point is it still acceptable to steal bases or take the extra base, and at what point do you risk offending the opponent to the point somebody might get hit?

"You can read body language of players," veteran outfielder Adam Eaton said. "Sometimes it depends on where it is in a season, whether runs are being readily scored or not readily scored. There's a lot that goes into it."

In this era where anyone can hit a home run, any team could come back. Should the Texas Rangers have stopped running and started going base-to-base on July 24, 2018? They led the Oakland A's 10–2 with nine outs to go.

They also lost the game, 13–12 in 10 innings.

The traditional rule was five runs late in the game, as Samuel said. The idea was that with a five-run lead, even a grand slam won't tie the game. And even though rates of scoring runs go up and down in different eras, many traditional baseball guys stuck to that number.

Not everyone does stick to it, and not everyone agrees what constitutes late in the game. In a game between the Diamondbacks and Twins in August 2017, Twins outfielder Byron Buxton took off for second with the Twins holding a 12–4 lead in the fifth inning. An inning later, D-Backs pitcher Braden Shipley nailed Twins catcher Chris Gimenez in the ribs.

It was only the fifth inning, but an eight-run lead is big at any point. On the other hand, Shipley had thrown over to first a few times, as Gimenez pointed out to reporters after the game.

"If you're going to [throw] over to first, I feel like you kind of have the right to steal," Gimenez said. "If that was the seventh inning, or sixth, seventh, eighth inning, I don't think he's going right there. But it is the fifth and if you're going to continue to pick over he's got every right to steal."

Rajai Davis, who had played for seven different major-league teams and had 415 career steals through 2018, said he always allowed his manager to decide how big a lead is too big when it came to shutting down the running game.

"It starts with your manager," Davis said. "You have an idea what's acceptable for your manager. I think everybody has their own opinion. Some say it's one more run than a grand slam [at any point], others say if it's the first three or four innings, it's fair game."

Davis' own feeling was based on the motivation. If you're running simply to build up stats, maybe it's not the right time to run. If you're running because that extra base helps your team's chances of winning, go right ahead and run.

So what about Lou Brock, who held the all-time record for career steals until Rickey Henderson broke it in 1991?

Brock is still tied with Eddie Collins for the career World Series record, with 14 steals in 1967–68. He tied Collins with a steal in the eighth inning of Game 4 in 1968... right after his three-run double had extended the Cardinal lead to 10–1.

That's right, Lou Brock stole third with a nine-run lead in the eighth inning. In the World Series.

If video replay had been in effect then, Brock might have been called out on the play. It was close enough at third that the Tigers argued umpire Tom Gorman's call. Meanwhile, in the NBC broadcast booth, Tigers announcer George Kell told his audience that the Tigers had to be upset with the timing, too, since Brock was running with a big lead.

Kell was right. The Tigers were upset. Because it was the World Series, they never threw at Brock in retaliation, and in that era before interleague play, Brock never faced the Tigers in a regular-season game in the years that followed.

But in his book, *Joy in Tigertown: A Determined Team, a Resilient City, and our Magical Run to the 1968 World Series*, Tigers pitcher

Mickey Lolich relayed a line second baseman Dick McAuliffe used at the time.

"That isn't the way the game should be played," McAuliffe said, according to Lolich.

Brock insisted he had done nothing wrong, even claiming after the game that the Tigers weren't upset. The Cardinals outfielder suggested that tying Collins' record was reason enough to run.

"I would not have tried to steal if I didn't have a record to shoot at," Brock told reporters. "After all, this could have been my last chance. I might never have another chance at a World Series. I owed it to myself."

He was right about one thing. It was Brock's last World Series. Brock had just one steal attempt in the final three games of the Series. Bill Freehan threw him out and he ended his World Series with 14 steals, still tied with Collins for the all-time record (through 2018, no active player had more than four).

While the Tigers never threw at Brock, Lolich wrote that the steal gave them more motivation to come back in the World Series.

And they did, getting their revenge on the field. Brock's steal came in Game 4, which the Cardinals won to extend their World Series lead to three games to one. They didn't win again, with the Tigers sweeping the final three games to win their first World Series title since 1945.

Brock went 5-for-12 in the final three games to finish with a .516 batting average. But he scored only one run in those three games, and he didn't steal another base. He also got thrown out at home plate in one of the biggest plays of Game 5, going in standing up as Freehan tagged him.

Three days before he stole third with a nine-run lead, Brock stole second base in Game 2 with the Cardinals trailing 6–1 in the eighth inning. That one caused a bit of a stir, too, when a Detroit newspaper quoted Lolich calling Brock a "showboat."

Other newspapers said at the time that Lolich did question Brock's timing, suggesting the steal was about calling attention to himself. Brock told reporters at the time that he simply was trying to rattle Lolich, who was dominating the Cardinals that day and would go on to win the Most Valuable Player Award when the Tigers won the World Series.

Lolich didn't get rattled by the steal, but he wasn't happy with the report that used the word "showboat."

In his book, Lolich said he called the Cardinals clubhouse the next day to speak with Brock directly.

"I told him not to believe the story," Lolich wrote. "He said he didn't."

Half a century later, there's still some question about when a big lead should stop a player from running. All-Star catcher Yadier Molina said if a baserunner wants to try to go, he won't complain.

"I don't get upset too often," Molina said. "They can do whatever they want. The game has changed. You have to adjust."

Not everyone feels the same way. In a May 2014 game at Tropicana Field, Rays shortstop Yunel Escobar was on second base after a seventh-inning double that put his team ahead of the Red Sox 8–3. When he noticed the Boston infielders weren't paying him much attention, Escobar took off for third. The official scorer didn't even award him a stolen base, calling it defensive indifference. But Red Sox catcher David Ross, who wasn't even in the game at the time, didn't like it. He yelled at Escobar from the third-base dugout and Escobar yelled back. Before long, Jonny Gomes had run in from left field and shoved Escobar. It wasn't the biggest brawl of all time, but it was enough to get Escobar, Gomes, and Rays utility man Sean Rodriguez (who had joined in) ejected from the game.

So did Escobar do anything wrong, running with a five-run lead in the seventh?

Red Sox manager John Farrell called it "somewhat of a gray area." Rays manager Joe Maddon defended his player and criticized the Red Sox for their reaction, correctly pointing out Jacoby Ellsbury stole second with an 8–2 eighth-inning lead against the Rays in the playoffs the previous October.

Four years later, it was the Rays who were upset about an opponent running with an 8–2 lead. It was June 6, 2018, and the Washington Nationals led the Rays by that score when Michael A. Taylor stole third base in the sixth inning with Sergio Romo on the mound.

Fast-forward 20 days. Romo was closing out a 1–0 Rays win over the Nationals at Tropicana Field. Taylor was the final batter and after Romo finished the game by striking him out, the Rays pitcher wagged his finger, stared down Taylor, and shouted at him all the way back to the Nationals dugout. The benches briefly emptied.

"No disrespect to that team," Romo said after the game. "No disrespect to that coaching staff. No disrespect to anybody on that team other than the person I felt disrespected me and my team."

Taylor's answer was simply that the game wasn't over at 8–2 in the sixth.

"Obviously, they think differently, but I'm not worried about that," Taylor told reporters.

A few weeks later, Romo explained that his understanding had always been that you don't run with a five-run lead after the fifth inning. If you do, you're only trying to pad your own statistics and being disrespectful.

Besides, Romo said, it's not like he threw at Taylor.

"There was never any intent to cause any harm," Romo said. "There was only an attempt to inform, to let him know. I don't know him personally. I don't have anything against him personally. But I didn't like what he did, and the first chance I had, I let him know.

"Did my point get made?"

51

When You Sit to Wear a Crown

TED WILLIAMS MADE HIS POINT IN A VERY DIFFERENT WAY
on the final day of the 1941 season.

Williams went into that final day batting .39955, which
would go into the books as .400 since batting averages are
always rounded to three places after the decimal point. He
could have sat out the Boston Red Sox's doubleheader that day
in Philadelphia. He could have sat after his second-inning single
in the first game, which raised his average to .40089. He could
have sat out the second game, which he began with a .404 average after going 4-for-5 in the opener.

Williams played both games. He came to the plate eight times.
He got six hits. He finished the season at .406, a number that
has only become more amazing by the year, since no one has
hit .400 in a season since then.

"If there's ever a player who deserved to hit .400, it's Ted,"
Red Sox manager Joe Cronin told reporters that day. "He's given
up plenty of chances to bunt and protect his average in recent

weeks. He wouldn't think of getting out of the lineup to keep his average intact."

The Red Sox were 18 games out of first place with a week to go in the season. They were well ahead of the third-place Chicago White Sox.

But when Cronin offered him the chance to sit, Williams declined. It wasn't that he didn't care about the stats. According to what he told others at the time and in later years, he cared very much. But he also cared about getting to .400 in what he felt was the right way.

"If I'm going to hit .400," he said, "I want more than my toe-nails on the line."

Compare that to what Jose Reyes did on the final day of the 2011 season. Reyes went into the day hitting .336, leaving him one point ahead of Milwaukee's Ryan Braun in the National League batting race. The Mets were playing an afternoon game at home against the Cincinnati Reds. The Brewers were at home for a night game against the Pittsburgh Pirates.

Reyes, whose season would be over before Braun took the field, decided a .337 average would be enough to get him the crown. If he went 1-for-1, he'd get to .337 and Braun would need to go 3-for-4 to beat him.

So that's what he was going to do.

Coming to the plate in the bottom of the first, Reyes put down a bunt and raced to first base. And as soon as he was called safe and had that .337 average in his pocket, he turned toward to the Mets' first-base dugout. Mets manager Terry Collins sent Justin

Turner to run for him, and the sparse crowd that had cheered Reyes' hit began to boo.

"To be honest with you," former Met Keith Hernandez said on the SNY television broadcast, "I am not going to agree with this move at all."

"I heard some comments in the stands," Collins said. "I don't blame them. People pay a good price to come to these games. You've got to understand that I ask these players to do a lot. We worked hard to get their respect this year, and they deserve ours."

Reyes said the fans "have to understand what's going on. They have to feel happy about it if I win the batting title. I do it for the team and for the fans, too."

There was plenty going on. Reyes was headed for free agency and would leave the Mets that winter. He left with the batting title, as it turned out, because Braun went 0-for-4 that night to finish the season at .332. But he left with a touch less respect, because of the way he won it.

Criticism of Reyes even came from other players.

C.J. Wilson, then pitching for the Rangers, took to Twitter and wrote: "Seriously people—taking out a star player to preserve his batting average lead...weak! I hope ryan braun goes 5-5 and wins the title now."

The reality is that managers and players often manipulate what happens in the final days of a season because of statistics. They do it to make sure a player stays over .300 for the season, or to give a pitcher an extra chance at a 20th win.

And sometimes they do it to give a guy a chance at a batting title.

Going into the final day of the 1982 season, Willie Wilson of the Kansas City Royals (.332) held a slim lead over Robin Yount (.328) in the American League batting race. Wilson sat out the Royals' final game of the season, saying, "My pride told me to play, but common sense told me not to."

But then Yount got three hits that day against the Baltimore Orioles. Suddenly he was hitting .331, just a point behind Wilson. In Kansas City, the Royals were getting nervous.

If Yount got one more hit, his average would be .33176, just a touch better than Wilson's .33162.

So with two out in the ninth in a meaningless game the 94-loss A's led 6–3, Oakland manager Billy Martin went to the mound and, according to reports, delayed the game for five minutes. His objective, according to what he told reporters that day? To waste time so the Royals could find out what Yount did in his final trip to the plate in Baltimore.

"I was buying time for Wilson," Martin said. "[Royals manager Dick] Howser called."

As it turned out, Yount was hit by a pitch in the ninth inning of a game the Brewers led 10–2 to clinch the American League East. He would finish at .33070. Martin could go back to the dugout and let Dave Beard get the final out.

Wilson could go to the Royals clubhouse to celebrate his batting title.

"I didn't want to win by sneaking in by the back door... but I did sneak in the back door," he told reporters after winning the closest batting race since 1949. "I'd like to have played... but I wanted to win the batting title more."

Yount went on to the playoffs and eventually to the World Series, where his Brewers lost to the St. Louis Cardinals. But first Brewers general manager Harry Dalton would express his indignation at what Martin and presumably Howser had done.

"Things like batting titles are supposed to be won in the process of winning ballgames for the team, and not by individual manipulation," Dalton told columnist Dick Young. "You're either good enough to win something or you're not."

Martin didn't seem too concerned about any of that, or about any sense of propriety in the final game of that season. He started outfielder Dwayne Murphy at shortstop, the only time in 12 major-league seasons Murphy started a game in the infield. He also played pitcher Rick Langford for one inning in center field and four innings in left field.

That's in the record books. So is Willie Wilson's batting title.

But if Wilson had anything to apologize for, he was hardly alone. Colorado Rockies manager Walt Weiss held Justin Morneau out of the lineup for the final two games of the 2014 season, helping Morneau hold off Josh Harrison and Andrew McCutchen for the National League batting crown.

"Anybody who has a problem with it, then their beef can be with me," Weiss told reporters. "I'm going to try and make sure the guy wins the batting title. People can talk about backing into it and stuff, but that doesn't bother me. It takes six months to win a batting title, not one day."

As it turned out, Morneau finished the season with exactly the same number of plate appearances as Harrison, who finished second. Does it really matter that only one of Morneau's plate appearances came in the final two games of the season? Is that any different from a manager sitting a guy midway through the year against a pitcher who always gives him trouble?

To some people it is different. Sitting a guy against a pitcher he doesn't hit is part of every season. It means giving the team a better chance to win, and picking a spot during a long season to give a star a rest.

It's not building your lineup around an individual honor.

The same weekend Morneau sat out in Los Angeles, Houston Astros interim manager Tom Lawless decided to leave Jose Altuve out of the lineup for the final game of the season in New York. Altuve had a three-point lead over Victor Martinez in the AL batting race.

Altuve talked his way into the lineup and went on to get two hits against the Mets, holding onto his lead over Martinez and winning the first batting title in Astros history.

"If you want to win something, you've got to win it on the field," Altuve told reporters.

Altuve did just that, as did Williams and as did Detroit Tigers Hall of Famer Harry Heilmann in 1925. Heilmann, who won four batting titles in his career, was battling Tris Speaker of the Indians for that season's crown. The Tigers had a doubleheader on the final day of the season, and after the first game Heilmann was ahead of Speaker, who wasn't playing that day.

Told he could win the crown by sitting out, Heilmann said: "Not me. I'll win it fairly, or not at all. I'll be in there swinging."

He was in there hitting. Heilmann went 3-for-3 in that final game, finishing the season at .393 to win the title.

52

There's No Need to Say You're Sorry

THERE WAS NO BATTING TITLE ON THE LINE AT AT&T PARK in San Francisco on the weekend before the All-Star break in 2018. But there sure was a lot of pride, especially for Oakland A's outfielder Mark Canha.

Canha grew up in San Jose, California, rooting for the San Francisco Giants. He was drafted by the Florida Marlins in 2010, taken (via trade) in the Rule 5 draft in 2014 by the A's. In the middle game of that 2018 series against the Giants, Canha came to the plate as a pinch hitter, in the seventh inning of a game the A's trailed 3–2.

On a 3-2 pitch from Giants reliever Tony Watson, Canha blasted a two-run home run that put the A's in front.

And yeah, he flipped his bat.

Nothing wrong with that. Huge moment, huge home run, and a celebration that fit.

So it was a little surprising when Canha offered an apology in his postgame interview.

"I'm sure a lot of San Franciscans are offended by that," he said. "And I'm sorry."

Fortunately, Canha wasn't done. He wasn't done flipping, and he wasn't done talking.

"You know what, people getting offended by bat flips is so silly," he said. "I'm not sorry. I'm not really sorry. It's part of our game. Everybody does it. If someone is going to throw at me because of it, I've got thrown at in the past this season for bat flipping. I clearly didn't learn my lesson. If you're offended by that, I don't care."

He shouldn't care and no one should be offended. The idea that a simple bat flip like Canha's "disrespected" Watson or the Giants is absurd. And to be fair, no Giants said or did anything to suggest they felt that way.

Former Giant pitcher Mike Krukow, the analyst for Giants games on CSN Bay Area, did say on his weekly radio show that he would have "moved [Canha's] feet" in a future at-bat. But even Krukow didn't seem that put out by Canha's celebration.

"I think guys in this generation, they've accepted it's part of it," said Krukow, who pitched in the big leagues from 1976 to 1989. "As to the comment that he made when he was walking back from home plate to the dugout about this being 'my house,' we kind of laughed about it. Like wait a second, this guy's a .230 hitter or something here in this ballpark. That ain't exactly putting up a flag saying it's my house. But he did hit the home run that gave his team the lead and eventually the win so he was feeling pretty froggy."

Krukow did lead the league in hit batters one year (with eight), so maybe he would have moved Canha's feet. Maybe in that era, Canha wouldn't have flipped the bat in the first place. But the idea that a hitter in 2018 should feel the need to apologize for flipping his bat after a huge game-turning home run in a rivalry game feels wrong.

And yet, Canha wasn't alone.

A month later, in a Sunday night game at Wrigley Field, Chicago Cubs rookie David Bote came to the plate in the ninth inning with the bases loaded and the Cubs down 3–0 to the Washington Nationals. Bote crushed a Ryan Madson pitch high over the center-field fence for a walkoff grand slam.

And yes, Bote celebrated by flipping his bat. Flipped it quite dramatically (a lot more dramatically than Canha did).

Why not?

Bote was just the 29th player in major-league history to erase a three-run lead with a walkoff grand slam. He was just the seventh to do it as a pinch hitter. And it was just his third major-league home run. And there were two out and two strikes.

He needed no apology. But he offered one in a way, the day after the slam, in an appearance on Chicago's 670 The Score radio.

"I didn't even realize I did it until I saw it on the replay," Bote said. "I thought, 'Oh man, I did bat flip it.' Obviously, I meant no disrespect by any means. It was just the heat of the moment, I got it good and I was wishing it out."

Of course he meant no disrespect. Of course he was excited. It was, as he said that night, a "magical" moment.

Not everyone would have reacted with a bat flip. Jason Heyward didn't flip his bat when he hit a walkoff grand slam for the Cubs that same season. Cubs third baseman Kris Bryant makes a point of never flipping his bat.

But Bote's flip was as natural as Kirk Gibson's famous double-fist pump in the 1988 World Series, as natural as Carlton Fisk waving his home run ball to stay fair in 1975. There was absolutely nothing wrong with it.

"Players should never apologize for bat flips," MLB.com's Alyson Footer wrote on Twitter after reading what Bote said. "They're glorious. Grumpy old men need to zip it. More bat flips, please."

To be fair, I'm not sure there were any grumpy old men complaining about what Bote did. But maybe there were.

The people who complain about bat flips mostly get upset after untimely flips. They roll their eyes when a player like Juan Soto flips after a walk, or when Odubel Herrera flips after doubles, singles, and sometimes even foul balls.

Pittsburgh Pirates manager Clint Hurdle complained about Cubs infielder Javier Baez after a game early in the 2018 season. Baez flipped his bat on a pop-up to shortstop against Hurdle's Pirates.

"You watch their kid flip that bat last night?" Hurdle asked reporters. "Where's the respect for the game? The guy hits four homers in two days, so that means you can take your bat and throw it 15, 20 feet in the air when you pop up like you should have hit your fifth home run? I would bet that men over there talked to him, because I do believe they have a group over there that speaks truth to power."

Baez took offense at Hurdle questioning the way he plays, but he agreed it wasn't the best situation for a flip.

"You know what I learned?" Baez said. "How ugly I looked on that fly ball. I tossed the bat really high, didn't run to first base and one of my teammates came up to me and said it, in a good way. You learn from it.... I was mad about it. Not the fly ball, just the way I looked for the kids and everyone that follows me. That's not a good look. I learned that from today."

Asked about it a couple months later, Hurdle said he wasn't completely comfortable criticizing a player on another team.

"It just came to a point where I was watching one of the most talented players in the game," Hurdle said. "He just hit four home runs against us in two days. And he popped up and there was a bat flip and I was just like, 'Wow.' For me, I wasn't just not going to say anything."

Hurdle said he would do the same with a player on his own team.

"I believe in playing with emotion," he said. "I don't believe in playing emotionally. I believe we all need to celebrate successes. When it's all about the event, okay. But when it's all about you performing the event, that's when we need to take a step back.

"I just think there's a respect for the game I'm trying to keep intact as long as I'm in uniform."

The celebrations can't get in the way of playing the game, as Cubs catcher Willson Contreras learned in the 2016 World Series. In the ninth inning of Game 1, with the Cubs down 6–0, he hit a ball to right field that he assumed was a home run. He took a couple of slow steps, then dramatically flipped his bat.

A bat flip down 6–0 in the ninth. A little much, but it is the World Series?

But the timing wasn't the problem. The problem was the ball didn't get out of the ballpark. So this wasn't about offending the opposition. It was about offending sensibilities.

This time, Contreras was absolutely right to say he was sorry, which he did via Twitter.

"I apologize to fans from both sides I didn't mean to disrespect My team @Cubs and the game!! Promise It Won't Happen Again," Contreras wrote.

Contreras didn't mean he was done flipping. He absolutely was not done flipping. Two years later, NBCSports.com dubbed him "King of the bat flip."

He even flipped after a home run in spring training. No apology needed.

And as for Canha and the A's, they had no intention of ever apologizing for a well-timed flip. They were even celebrating their celebratory flips.

Canha had T-shirts made that he gave to his teammates and sold to fans. The shirts had his name and his likeness and three big words:

"Bat Flippin' Season."

53

It's the Players
Who Police the Game

WHETHER IT'S WITH RULES ABOUT COLLISIONS AT SECOND
base or home plate or with heavy suspensions and fines for
pitchers throwing at hitters or hitters charging the mound, those
who run baseball have tried to take some decisions away from
the guys who play the game.

The guys who play the game don't always like it.

They'll tell you that the players are perfectly capable of policing the game themselves, that they understand better than anyone what is acceptable and what isn't.

"I'm not big on making the game better by adding more reg-
ulations," Colorado Rockies outfielder Charlie Blackmon said.
"Let's let the guys play the game."

He's not alone, and old-time players like to tell stories about
how they took care of issues on the field themselves, rather than
asking an umpire or the league office for help.

When Sergio Romo was a little too demonstrative on the
mound early in his career and opponents responded by throwing

at his teammates, Romo learned his lesson. Tone it down a little, so you don't get any of your teammates hurt.

In other cases, players who felt wronged found ways to take action themselves.

Juan Samuel remembers one time he was sliding head-first into second base, and Jose Oquendo dropped his knee onto Samuel's arm.

"I got up and told him if you do that again, I'll punch you right here," Samuel said.

But that's not the only thing Samuel did.

"The next time I got on base, I took a big old lead to see if he did it again, and I went feet-first," he said.

Drop your knee this time and you'll find my spikes stuck in you. But Oquendo had heeded the warning. He didn't drop his knee.

Other baserunners from that era will tell you similar stories with other infielders. Infielders will tell stories of runners coming in to break up a double play with their head held high to disrupt a throw.

Throw it right at them, the infielders were taught. They won't come in that way again.

"We used to stick up for ourselves," Samuel said.

That's one of the things players mean when they say the game will police itself. Players let other players know when they've strayed, and the lessons are learned quickly and thoroughly.

Sometimes that meant a batter charging the mound when he thought a pitcher was throwing at him. Players told other players that they didn't want to see them just chirping at a pitcher.

Either you can take action or not. Just don't waste everyone's time talking about it.

"I've always been taught if you're going to do something about it, do it," veteran outfielder Adam Eaton said. "And if you're not, why are you going to sit there and chirp like a dog over a fence. I'm not about that. If I'm going to go, I'm going to go. And if I'm not, I'm not."

Eaton was talking a day after he believed strongly that the New York Mets had intentionally thrown at him twice, in retaliation for a hard slide breaking up a double play a few weeks earlier. One of the pitches from Zack Wheeler sailed up and in. Another hit Eaton in the rear end, and rather than respond to it in any way, Eaton quietly took his base.

But Eaton wasn't looking to Nationals manager Dave Martinez to decide whether baseball justice needs to be applied. That applies to charging the mound and also to whether a team needs to retaliate by hitting someone on the other team.

"I don't think it's up to the manager," Eaton said. "If it's a manager's decision, then the manager has too much control of the clubhouse. Guys police themselves. Pitchers police themselves, a lot of veteran pitchers and position players. And that's not just about pitchers hitting people. Like with [19-year-old outfielder] Juan Soto, Skip's not going to his room making sure he's tucked in his bed at night.

"The skipper manages people. He manages the lineup. Players have a job to do as well."

This is professional baseball, after all. Players are adults, and they expect the manager to treat them that way. A manager does set out the way he expects his team to play and act, but every good manager understands a team operates more effectively if the players handle issues before those issues ever come to him.

54

Baseball Is Still a Game
of Numbers

THE NIGHT BLAKE SNELL BECAME BASEBALL'S FIRST 20-GAME
winner of 2018 (and the Tampa Bay Rays' first 20-game winner
in six years), Tyler Kepner of the *New York Times* saluted Snell
on Twitter.

"Blake Snell, 20-game winner," he wrote. "No apologies—I still
think a 20-win season is pretty cool."

So do I, but I also know that in this era it's not always
considered "cool" to believe that. The cool kids follow MLB
Network's Brian Kenny, whose mantra for several years has
been Kill the Win.

In some ways, his reasoning makes perfect sense. The scoring rule that assigns wins to individual pitchers has always had
quirks that made it imperfect. Assigning wins to relievers never
really fit, because in far too many cases the win ended up going
to someone whose main contribution to the game was to sur-
render the lead handed him by the starter, only to become the
pitcher of record when his team re-took the lead. Even assigning

wins to starters became less palatable in an era when starting pitchers are in the game for fewer and fewer innings.

When Denny McLain won 31 games in 1968, he only needed help from his bullpen three times. That's right, of McLain's 31 wins, 28 were complete games. While he needed help from his hitters and his defense, calling him the winning pitcher was hardly out of line.

At the time he won 20 games, Snell had never thrown a complete game. Not once, in 72 career starts. It wasn't his fault, and it doesn't make him a lesser pitcher. He's the product of his era, and that era (and his team) rarely allow a pitcher to go nine innings. The Rays had two complete games in the last four seasons combined.

In half of his first 20 wins of 2018, Snell didn't throw a pitch after the sixth inning. The night he won his 20th, Rays manager Kevin Cash pulled him after just five innings, even though he'd allowed just one hit and no runs. Again, not his fault, except that he threw 92 pitches in those five innings, and in today's world that can be a red flag even for a pitcher who is otherwise dominating.

We don't have accurate pitch counts for 1968, but newspaper reports said McLain threw 229 pitches in one complete-game win in 1966. He walked nine and struck out 11, and decades before anyone talked about the "third time through the order," he faced the best of the Baltimore Orioles hitters five times and allowed just three runs.

Can anyone really say McLain didn't earn a "win" that day?

If you want to argue that wins are no longer predictive of future success, or even that they never were predictive, that's fine. If you want to argue that Jacob deGrom pitched tons better than his 10–9 record in 2018 and that wins don't do him justice, well, you're right.

Wins don't tell the whole story. They never did. They're not the best stat to predict who will succeed in the future. They never were.

But they do help tell the story of what happened in a season, and just as no one wins a home run title by hitting only cheap home runs, no one puts together a 20-win season with only cheap wins. Snell needed help from his teammates, but he also had to be consistently good over six months. He needed them to make plays for him and score runs for him, but he had to pitch well enough to make those plays and those runs add up to wins.

He didn't have 41 starts, as McLain did in 1968, because teams no longer use a four-man rotation. He had to rely on his bullpen, because teams no longer allow starters to routinely throw complete games no matter the pitch count. What Snell had to do was put himself in position where he could get credit for 20 wins, if the other factors went his way.

He put himself in position. Things went his way. In a game where there's a winner and a loser, his team won a lot more often than it lost when he was pitching.

There's nothing wrong with adding that up. There's nothing wrong with adding up the number of home runs one player hits, the number of runs that score as a result of one players' hits (a simple way to describe RBI).

Count them up and celebrate the big numbers. It's part of what most of us grew to love about the game.

It's equally true that in the modern game, we have other numbers that dive deeper to tell which player performed better. Many of those numbers are worth looking at, too. When I had a vote for MVP or Rookie of the Year, I wanted to see who was leading in WAR and wOBA and OPS+, which attempt to give more of an overall picture to a hitter's season. I looked at WHIP for pitchers, and at walk rates and strikeout rates and the number of home runs allowed.

I didn't have a Cy Young vote in 2018, but if I'd had that vote in the National League, deGrom would have been first on my ballot, despite his low win total. I would have voted for Snell first in the American League, not solely because of his wins but because his overall season made him the best choice.

Wins aren't a "completely arbitrary number," as one commenter on Twitter claimed when I joined Kepner in celebrating Snell's 20-win accomplishment. You can believe they don't have the significance they once did and still think they're worth counting, noting, and even celebrating when one pitcher gets a whole bunch of them.

That goes for Snell and his 20 wins, and for Bartolo Colon and the 244 career wins he needed to pass Juan Marichal for the most ever by a pitcher born in the Dominican Republic. It goes for Justin Verlander, who got his 200th career win in 2018, leaving him right about where Nolan Ryan was after his age-35 season.

Could Verlander pitch until he's 46, as Ryan did, and get to 300 wins, as Ryan did?

If he does, I'll be watching. And if Brian Kenny doesn't want to watch with me, he's more than welcome to calculate instead what effect those extra years and games are having on Verlander's career WAR.

55

When It Comes Down to It, It's Still about Playing the Game Right

EARLY IN THE 2018 SEASON, VETERAN SECOND BASEMAN Ian Kinsler was talking about how the game has changed.

"If anything, analytics is through the roof," he said. "It's kind of a joke, really."

He's not alone in thinking that and I understand what he means, even if I don't agree at all that the numbers and numbers people are ruining the game. Shifts make sense. Bunting a lot less frequently makes sense. Using every bit of information available to try to win a game is exactly what managers and players did years ago, with the only difference being there's plenty more information available and plenty of smart people willing to figure out how to best use it.

At the same time, the games are won by the best players most of the time.

"When it comes down to it, the game's about execution," Kinsler said. "You can have an opener, like Tampa did, because of some statistic, but if the hitters execute at the plate and the pitcher doesn't, it's not going to work. It doesn't matter what the stats say. That's why baseball is special, because there can be a stat that says this guy hasn't hit a homer off this pitcher for 30 at-bats, and then he hits a homer."

I know exactly what he means by that.

In May 1991, I was covering a game at Tiger Stadium between the Detroit Tigers and the Boston Red Sox. Roger Clemens was on the mound for the Sox, at a time when he was without much argument the best pitcher in the game. He was in the middle of a stretch where he would finish in the top three in American League Cy Young voting five times in seven years. He won it three times, including that season.

He was tough for anyone to hit, but even the rudimentary numbers available back then told us he was near-impossible for Pete Incaviglia to hit. Incaviglia had been to the plate nine times against Clemens in his career. Each and every one of those nine times, Clemens struck him out.

A manager today would look at those numbers and decide a game against Clemens was a good time to give Incaviglia a night off.

Sparky Anderson made him the designated hitter.

It didn't look good when Clemens struck out Incaviglia in his first two at-bats, running their personal head-to-head record to 0-for-11 with 11 Ks. But in the seventh inning of a game that was tied 2–2, Incaviglia ripped a double to left field to put the Tigers ahead.

They went on to win the game.

"I don't believe in that stuff," Sparky had said before the game, when we asked why Incaviglia was in the lineup against a guy the numbers said he couldn't hit. "Every night is a different night. Those numbers, that's the biggest and silliest thing. Guys use computers instead of keeping it up here in their head. You watch the game with your eyes."

You watch the game with your eyes, and when you watch it today you're seeing some of the best players who ever played.

"I think we're in the golden era of baseball right now," Kinsler said. "Absolutely. The things that are happening on the field every night [are] ridiculous. It's harder to get a base hit, but there's still guys that are hitting [.350]. Power numbers are as good as ever. Strikeout numbers. Athleticism is better. There's more ground being covered. It's a great game right now, and people lose sight of what's actually happening on the field. They want to know what the next great thing is. Well, there's a great thing every night."

At the time we spoke, Kinsler was playing for the Los Angeles Angels, where he was teammates with Mike Trout and Shohei Ohtani, the new pitching and hitting sensations. Later in the year, he was traded to the Boston Red Sox, where he was teammates with Mookie Betts and J.D. Martinez and would win a World Series for the first time in his career.

"If your view of the game is that it's boring, then you probably shouldn't watch it," he said. "I'm not going to watch something if I think it's boring. I'll flip the channel. If you don't like it, don't watch it. There's plenty of people watching it."

And there are still plenty of players and teams who understand what it means to play the game right.

ACKNOWLEDGMENTS

THE DAY AFTER I SENT IN THE MANUSCRIPT FOR THIS BOOK, the Oakland A's announced that reliever Liam Hendriks would start the American League Wild Card Game at Yankee Stadium. The next day, the Milwaukee Brewers announced they would use an opener in Game 1 of the National League Division Series against the Colorado Rockies.

"We're trying to get away from what the words 'starter' and 'reliever' mean," Counsell said.

A day after that, Justin Verlander took a no-hitter into the sixth inning and was out of the game one out later, before he'd even allowed a run.

"*They're going to get him?*" Dennis Eckersley screamed into his TBS microphone.

Yes, the game is changing. In reality, it's changing all the time. It always has.

The idea of this book was to figure out how those changes affect the unwritten rules. How is the game played today? What does it look like? What can you do that you may not have been able to do years ago? And what seems like it has changed but really hasn't?

Thankfully, people around baseball love talking about all of that. For nearly two seasons, while working on this book, I got input from players, coaches, managers, executives, scouts, broadcasters, and even other writers. Some of them are quoted in these pages. Some just shared a few of their thoughts and observations.

Most of them added that they love the subject.

Arizona Diamondbacks coach Jerry Narron told me that he'd read how Frank Crosetti almost never shook a home run hitter's hand when he coached third base for the New York Yankees for 37 years. I looked it up and he was right; according to the obituary Bill Madden wrote in 2002 in the *New York Daily News*:

"Crosetti was noted for never shaking hands with a player who had just hit a home run. Instead, he would merely pat him on the back. However, Crosetti made an exception to that rule when Mickey Mantle hit his mammoth home run off the Cardinals' Barney Schultz in the 1964 World Series."

That anecdote didn't even make it into the book—until now.

There were so many others from so many people. There was so much I learned from Sparky Anderson in my early years covering the Detroit Tigers, and also plenty I learned from Jim Leyland in my final years on the Tigers beat.

Among current managers, Joe Maddon, Gabe Kapler, Clint Hurdle, Kevin Cash, Don Mattingly, Brian Snitker, Terry

Francona, Dave Roberts, Torey Lovullo, Ron Gardenhire, Bud Black, and Bob Melvin all provided insight. So did current and former managers and coaches Juan Samuel, Mike Matheny, Doug Brocail, Phil Nevin, John Gibbons, Mike Scioscia, Perry Hill, Ron Washington, Lloyd McClendon, Chuck Hernandez, Walt Weiss, Kirk Gibson, and Brad Mills. Former players Gregg Olson, Alan Trammell, Jack Morris, David Cone, John Smoltz, Ray Fosse, Buck Martinez, Jim Price, David Wells, John McDonald, Steve Sparks, C.J. Nitkowski, Matt Keough, Rick Sutcliffe, and Ron Darling shared insights. So did current major leaguers, including Justin Verlander, Gerrit Cole, Ian Kinsler, Justin Upton, Martin Prado, Freddie Freeman, Kenley Jansen, Kenta Maeda, Yasiel Puig, Brad Ziegler, Peter Moylan, Archie Bradley, Jason Heyward, Kris Bryant, Max Scherzer, Gio Gonzalez, and Jose Bautista.

I talked unwritten rules with former big leaguer Gregg Zaun and while his words aren't in this book, those conversations helped me figure out some of my own views.

Those views go back decades, to growing up in Los Angeles. Vin Scully won deserved plaudits for the way he called baseball games, but those of us who were raised with the Dodgers of the 1960s and '70s remember how he also taught us the game. On those nights when we went to bed with a transistor radio under the pillow—yes, we really did. On those mornings we snuck radios into school to listen to the first spring games from Vero Beach (sorry, teachers, we did that, too).

I learned from Vin, and I learned from my father, who would take me to a few games a season at Dodger Stadium and explain what was going on down there on the field. I learned from Gary

Adams and Glenn Mickens and others at UCLA, and from Vern Plagenhoef, who understood the game better than any writer I know and who I was fortunate enough to work with at Booth Newspapers.

Now, all these years later, my father and mother and my brother are the best editors I have. If you find any errors in here, those are all mine. So are the ones my family caught before they made it into print.

What they didn't catch, Jesse Jordan did. I worked with Jesse and all the fine folks at Triumph Books on my first book, *Numbers Don't Lie.* I was thrilled when they wanted to work with me again, and with how Jesse helped shape this book.

Thanks also go to Josh Williams, Noah Amstadter, and Tom Bast, and to everyone else that make Triumph such a pleasant company to work with.

I never forget how fortunate I've been to make a career out of writing about baseball, and for the last five seasons much of that writing has appeared at Bleacher Report. In a business that continues to get more difficult, people like Stephen Meyer, Jake Leonard, Bill Eichenberger, Paul Forrester, and Mark Smoyer make Bleacher Report an outlier for giving us the space, time, and leadership to seek out and pursue the interesting stories that make baseball the best game of all to write about.

And, of course, working for Bleacher Report has given me more chances to collaborate with Scott Miller. We've been friends for years and professional colleagues since Scott helped bring me to CBSSports.com in 2008, and I couldn't have picked anyone better to work with.

I couldn't have picked anyone better to share this last decade with than my wife, Lek. Just as I wrote in the acknowledgements for the first book, she was always patient every time I told her I needed to "tahm ngahn" on the book.

SOURCES

BASEBALL HAS CHANGED OVER THE YEARS, AND IN THE pages of this book I've explained how and why some of those changes have happened. Baseball writing has also changed, and some of those changes helped make this book possible.

Start with Baseball-Reference.com, the website Sean Forman debuted in April 2000, because nearly everything we do begins there. Whether it's to simply look up a player's career record or to do a detailed search through the wonderful Play Index, Sean's site has become indispensable. Most of the stats listed in this book either come from Baseball Reference or were checked through Baseball Reference.

MLB.com's Statcast is quickly becoming every bit as essential, especially with the work Daren Willman has done with his BaseballSavant.com website. Daren's site was a great help in writing about shifts and pitch velocities, among other things, and he keeps adding more and more goodies.

Other statistics come from Fangraphs.com, BaseballProspectus.com, and BrooksBaseball.net.

Baseball history is about more than just numbers, and several other books and websites provided access to quotes and information that helped describe many of the unwritten rules of the game and how they've been applied. MLB.com provides a good record of recent events and even the ability to view entire games. The *New York Times* archive at Nytimes.com helped with many quotes from the pre-Internet age, as did the archives at the Newspapers.com site.

I also referenced these books in telling the story of baseball's unwritten rules:

Cepeda, Orlando, and Fagen, Herb. *Baby Bull: From Hardball to Hard Time and Back.* Taylor Trade Publishing. 1998.

Lolich, Mickey, with Tom Gage. *Joy in Tigertown: A Determined Team, a Resilient City and our Magical Run to the 1968 World Series.* Triumph Books. 2018.

Verducci, Tom. *The Cubs Way: The Zen of Building the Best Team in Baseball and Breaking the Curse.* Crown Archetype. 2017.

Francona, Terry, and Shaughnessy, Dan. *The Red Sox Years.* Houghton Mifflin Harcourt. 2013.

Ritter, Lawrence S. *The Glory of Their Times: The Story of the Early Days of Baseball Told by the Men Who Played It.* Harper Perennial. 1966.

Prager, Joshua. *The Echoing Green.* Pantheon. 2006.

Abbott, Jim and Brown, Tim. *Imperfect: An Improbable Life.* Ballantine Books. 2012.

Kenny, Brian. *Ahead of the Curve: Inside the Baseball Revolution.* Simon & Schuster. 2016.

Weaver, Earl, with Terry Pluto. *Weaver on Strategy: The Classic Work on the Art of Managing a Baseball Team.* Simon & Schuster. 1984.